Preparing for Educational Leadership: A Study Guide for Success in Taking Educational Leadership Licensure Examinations

Kenneth Forman, Ph.D.
Jeffrey Soloff

D1567468

Learning Solutions

New York   Boston   San Francisco
London   Toronto   Sydney   Tokyo   Singapore   Madrid
Mexico City   Munich   Paris   Cape Town   Hong Kong   Montreal

Pearson Learning Solutions, 501 Boylston Street, Suite 900, Boston, MA 02116
A Pearson Education Company
www.pearsoned.com

Printed in the United States of America

1 2 3 4 5 6 7 8 9 10 XXXX 14 13 12 11 10 09

000200010270561944

MP

ISBN 10: 0-558-68643-5
ISBN 13: 978-0-558-68643-7

Acknowledgements

We wish to gratefully acknowledge the time and energy our colleagues gave us during the editing process to validate case studies and short answer questions: Al Bauer, Melissa Kreiger, Terry O'Connor, Mark Rosenbaum, Frank Ruggiero, and Ed Sallie. We thank you all for your input without which we could never have proceeded with all due diligence and produced this book with the high level of accuracy it contains.

We wish to gratefully acknowledge the patience and understanding our wives gave us to make this book happen. Living with us is never easy, but our wives deserve medals for living with us as we wrote this book.

About the Authors

Dr. Kenneth Forman

Dr. Forman started his career in education as a middle school science teacher for the NYC public schools. He has served as middle school assistant principal, federal programs coordinator, director of state and federal programs, director of curriculum and instruction, executive assistant to the superintendent, assistant superintendent, and principal while working in the NYC public schools for 27 years. Additionally, he has served as elementary school principal in the Lawrence Public Schools for the last 12 years. He is currently a lecturer at Stony Brook University, Educational Leadership Program and consultant for Pearson Evaluation Systems.

Dr. Forman is a graduate of Queens College, Brooklyn College, and received his doctorate from New York University in Educational Administration.

Dr. Forman is also a consultant for the Division of Accountability and Achievement Resources, where he works with colleagues to review schools across New York City.

Mr. Jeffrey Soloff

Mr. Soloff earned his certificate in educational administration, masters in education, and bachelors' degree from Brooklyn College. His professional interests include developing a cadre of future school leaders and performing Quality Reviews in New York City public schools. Jeffrey has been an adjunct professor of educational leadership at Stony Brook University in New York since 2001. He teaches courses in leadership theory, leadership practice, building administration, and supervises administrative interns.

His career began in 1971 as an elementary school teacher. He assumed a variety of administrative positions at the building and district levels during the next eight years. Jeffrey spent nineteen years as an elementary school principal in New York City and in the Plainedge School District in North Massapequa, New York.

Jeffrey's twenty-seven years of administrative experience in public schools have given him a vast amount of knowledge and expertise that he has incorporated into this book.

Preface

Those who hire educational leaders usually thrust them into conditions that require a skill set that prospective leaders have not honed. Educational leaders often come from teaching ranks. Professional leadership programs try their best to prepare those candidates for success. However, no program can prepare the candidate for the intensity of instant decision making required to be a building or district level leader. We are sharing our sixty years of expertise and varied experiences in the case studies and "in-basket" exercises provided in this book. We hope to help you, the prospective educational leader, understand the complexity of leadership and the daily decision-making required for success. The Educational Testing Service and Pearson Education are the two major testing and evaluation companies that provide assessments for prospective administrators. Both tests require candidates to make quick decisions based upon a skill set of state and/or national standards for educational leaders. We used sample questions found on the test preparation websites of both companies as models in creating testing scenarios. We believe this preparation material will be helpful for you the candidate to be successful during the assessment process.

School leadership in the United States has coalesced around a set of standards, the ISLLC (Interstate School Leaders Licensure Consortium) standards, with 35 states adopting them. ISLLC, the Interstate School Leaders Licensure Consortium Standards were developed by the Council of Chief State School Officers to help strengthen preparation programs in school leadership in 1996. The other set of standards, ELCC, the Educational Leadership Constituents Council standards, were published in January 2002. The National Council for the Accreditation of Teacher Education (NCATE) used ISLLC standards to develop ELCC (Educational Leadership Constituents Council) standards. Candidates for principal licensure nationwide may be required to take ISLLC or ELCC based licensing examinations. Professional licensure programs revised their curricula to be in alignment with either ISLLC or ELCC standards. Organizations such as the National Association of State Boards of Education (NASBE) have openly recommended the use of the ISLLC standards by their membership. This does not mean ELCC Standards are not worthwhile; they definitely are. They are quite literally parallel to the ISLLC standards as illustrated below. However, ISLLC standards are the only common set of standards developed by a national body of state departments of education (originally 23 states) and national leadership organizations. Originally, 12 states were included as the members of National Policy Board for Educational Administration (NPBEA). Standards were designed for all school leaders, pre-K through 12, and were universally accepted and recognized. National membership organizations, such as the National Association of Elementary School Principals (NAESP), the National Association of Secondary School Principals (NASSP), and the American Association of School Administrators (AASA), all use the ISLLC standards. Both sets of standards developed for educational administration programs are parallel so that our case analyses and discussions are organized by ELCC standards. We think it is important that in order to resolve each problem, some basic facts should be established which helps to clarify the solution of the case. Assessment systems try to ascertain a potential administrator's knowledge in relation to a set of standards.

Standard 1:
- ELCC: Candidates who complete the program are educational leaders who have the knowledge and ability to promote the success of all students by facilitating the development, articulation, implementation, and stewardship of a school or district vision of learning supported by the school community.
- ISLCC: A school administrator is an educational leader who promotes the success of all students by facilitating the development, articulation, implementation, and stewardship of a vision of learning that is shared and supported by the school community.

Standard 2:
- ELCC: Candidates who complete the program are educational leaders who have the knowledge and ability to promote the success of all students promoting a positive school culture, providing an effective instructional program, applying best practice to student learning, and designing comprehensive professional growth plans for staff.
- ISLCC: A school administrator is an educational leader who promotes the success of all students by advocating, nurturing, and sustaining a school culture and instructional program conducive to student learning and staff professional growth.

Standard 3:
- ELCC: Candidates who complete the program are educational leaders who have the knowledge and ability to promote the success of all students by managing the organization, operations, and resources in a way that promotes a safe, efficient, and effective learning environment.
- ISLCC: A school administrator is an educational leader who promotes the success of all students by ensuring management of the organization, operations, and resources for a safe, efficient, and effective learning environment.

Standard 4:
- ELCC: Candidates who complete the program are educational leaders who have the knowledge and ability to promote the success of all students by collaborating with families and other community members, responding to diverse community interests and needs, and mobilizing community resources.
- ISLCC: A school administrator is an educational leader who promotes the success of all students by collaborating with families and community members, responding to diverse community interests and needs, and mobilizing community resources.

Standard 5:
- ELCC: Candidates who complete the program are educational leaders who have the knowledge and ability to promote the success of all students by acting with integrity, fairly, and in an ethical manner.
- ISLCC: A school administrator is an educational leader who promotes the success of all students by acting with integrity, fairness, and in an ethical manner.

Standard 6:
- ELCC: Candidates who complete the program are educational leaders who have the knowledge and ability to promote the success of all students by understanding, responding to, and influencing the larger political, social, economic, legal, and cultural context.
- ISLCC: A school administrator is an educational leader who promotes the success of all students by understanding, responding to, and influencing the larger political, social, economic, legal, and cultural context.

Educational leadership requires that individuals make decisions on an on-going basis and usually in rapid-fire succession. Therefore, this book will provide the opportunity for individuals to practice decision-making skills as well as sharpening test-taking strategies. We have divided the book into three sections, multiple choice questions, case studies, and work products. The case studies chapters include responses to typical educational decision-making cases that might be found in licensure examinations by ISLLC standards. Being successful during any written examination requires that the candidate rapidly and accurately size up a problem presented and make a judgment based upon facts presented in a particular case while considering a variety of alternate solutions. Cases provided are all real life situations that we have had to resolve over our many years as building and district level administrators. Responses to cases reflect what test administrators might ask of candidates taking these exams. Both ETS and Pearson provide samples of questions and model responses for prospective administrators' review. We have included three scenarios for your consideration in resolving cases included in this book.

- Scenario 1: (1) establish one strength of the administrator, (2) give one strategy for building on this strength, (3) specify one weakness of the administrator, (4) give a strategy for addressing that weakness, and (5) knowing this information, why might this strategy be effective in resolving the case.

- Scenario 2: (1) what did the administrator do well, (2) what did the administrator do poorly, (3) three actions the administrator might take to resolve the problem, and (4) why each action is likely to be effective.

- Scenario 3: (1) identify two key issues in the case, (3) give one strategy you might employ to resolve each issue identified, and (3) explain how that strategy might be effective in resolving the issues.

All case studies are authentic and have been validated by colleagues and field-tested by students in the Stony Brook Educational Leadership Program. Case studies in chapters 1–6 are categorized by standard and are either school-based or district-based situations.

Likewise, in Chapter 7 we provide you with a number of multiple choice questions organized by standards and are either school-based or district-based problems. Multiple-choice questions came from our everyday experiences as successful building or district administrators. Candidates must employ quick decision-making skills to make a sound educational decision in each example. Educational leaders face many situations each day that require immediate action. Sound judgment, knowledge, and experience factor into making good decisions. We ask that you read each question, think about possible alternatives, and make a decision to resolve the problem presented in the question. We then provide you with a solution and a rationale for making a particular decision. Multiple-choice questions are likewise divided into school-based and district-based questions.

In chapter 8, we provide you with two work products: one involving a school-based problem and another involving a district-based problem. Work products are similar to case studies. Both require careful analysis. However, in a work product, the candidate is given a variety of supplementary information attached to the problem, which requires interpretation and response. We feel it is important for candidates to develop a competency in reading and reacting to information provided through looking at a variety of documents and making informed judgments about particular situations.

We would like briefly to discuss test-taking strategies. Since the examination is given on the computer, you can decide on the order you wish to respond to the test questions. We believe that you should consider completing the essays first since they require extensive time for appropriate and comprehensive completion. When writing your response, it might be helpful if you outline for yourself the components of the response you want to include in your essay. Respond exactly as the question requires and in the order of the question components. Introductory and concluding paragraphs are nice, but only set the stage for the sections of required response. After you complete the essay, re-read it making sure that you responded exactly as required by the specific component of the question. If you provide additional information in your response, you demonstrate your mastery of the topic, which may be helpful in distinguishing a high quality response from a satisfactory response. Some essay questions ask the examinee to include assumptions, if any, that may influence the way in which an essay is read.

In responding to short answer questions, most short answer questions are structured so that two of the four answer choices are possible correct responses. Learn to find the inappropriate choices, exclude them from consideration, and then decide which of the two possible remaining responses best fits the question. Remember your first choice for a response is mostly likely the correct response for that question.

Table of Contents

Chapter 1

Standard 1: *to develop, articulate, implement, and steward a vision of learning*

Chapter 1

Standard 1: *to develop, articulate, implement, and steward a vision of learning*

School based case studies:

Case 1

You are the principal of a middle school in an affluent community where parents are extremely active and involved. The president of the Parent Organization has advised you that there are a number of very vocal parents who have "heard" that the middle school is adopting the International Baccalaureate program and "doing away with honors." They are angry and upset that their children might be mixed in with the general population and not get the special treatment. Parents felt that their children would not receive the challenging work that they have always enjoyed and would be asked to "help" or tutor the slower students in their classes. Another group of less-vocal parents heard the same rumor and became angry that their "average" children will now have incredible pressure to be "honors" and will have to take all the "International Baccalaureate tests." You have scheduled a parents' meeting to discuss this issue.

Directions:

Read the case carefully, and respond using scenario 1: (1) establish one strength of the administrator, (2) give one strategy for building on this strength, (3) indicate one weakness of the administrator, (4) give a strategy for addressing that weakness, and (5) knowing this information, why might these strategies be effective in resolving the case.

Response:

(1) The principal's strength in this case is recognition that pushing for higher levels of instruction is paramount and by implementing the International Baccalaureate program the expectations for success is high. Additionally, by recognizing there is a conflict among the parent population, the principal has decided to address this issue head on by meeting with all parents to discuss the pros and cons of the International Baccalaureate program.

(2) A strategy for building on this strength includes meeting with all constituencies before the group meeting to understand the issue from each group's perspective. Groups of parents, teachers, and building/district

level administrators should have an opportunity to offer their opinions. Additionally, if the principal has researched International Baccalaureate programs by speaking with administrators from existing schools with International Baccalaureate programs, the principal is aware of International Baccalaureate's strengths, weaknesses, and the issues they faced when the other schools introduced the program. Moreover, if the principal made the Superintendent aware of the forthcoming parent meeting, he could brainstorm several scenarios with him to address parent concerns.

(3) One weakness of the administrator is that the principal listened to the Parent Organization president's concern and assumed that she was representing all parents. The principal failed to sample other parents for their views.

(4) A strategy for addressing that weakness might include asking the Parent Organization president to have a variety of parents speak with him to verify that the concern was widespread. The principal also could survey all parents by sending a letter home asking for their input.

(5) The effect of this strategy would be that the principal would be able to speak directly to the different constituencies, determine their positions, and get a better idea of their concerns.

Case 2

The Jackson Elementary School has an enrollment of 650 students in grades K–5. It is one of three elementary schools in the district. The school has a principal, assistant principal, Parent Teacher Association, and a School Improvement Committee consisting of the principal, parents, and teachers. The school receives Title I funds that are used for remedial reading and math classes. There is a gifted and talented program as well as classes for children with limited English proficiency. There are two self-contained special education classes as well an "inclusion" class on each grade level. There is a resource room teacher, a speech teacher, and part-time occupational and physical therapists. The maximum class sizes are as follows: K & 1 – 22, 2 & 3 – 25, 4 & 5 – 30. The school has an excellent reputation in a community that emphasizes education. It is clean, well organized, and has a stable teaching staff. The school has an above average mobility rate. Recent test data in reading and math, however, indicates that students are not making adequate progress as far as test scores are concerned. In fact, scores have been slightly declining over the past three years in grades 3, 4, and 5; grade 2 scores are flat. The School Improvement Committee has been charged with examining the inadequate achievement scores. The teachers on the committee feel there is nothing they can do to improve achievement due to the unmotivated behavior of students in the school. The teachers on the committee have also indicated that the staff is hard working and maintains excellent discipline. The parents have been supportive of teacher efforts. The Superintendent called the principal into his office to express his dissatisfaction with the school's achievement scores and has required the principal to improve test scores.

Directions:

Read the case carefully, and respond using scenario 3: (1) identify two key issues in the case, (2) give one strategy you might employ to resolve each issue identified, and (3) explain how that strategy might be effective in resolving the issues.

Response:

(1) Two key issues in this case are:
- Teacher attitude towards student achievement is negative.
- The instructional program may not meet students' needs.

(2) A strategy that the principal might employ to resolve each issue is:

The principal should meet with teachers by grade levels and in committees to discuss student expectations and desired learning outcomes for students. The principal might establish learning communities to look at a variety of successful schools that have similar backgrounds to establish what works and what does not work in improving student achievement. Looking at best practices reinforces that children can learn. Once best practices are established, discussions might evolve into demonstration programs that staff might observe and consider for implementation. Therefore, by looking at what works in other places, the principal and work groups would attain a better understanding of what might work in their learning environment. Additionally, the principal might establish a data analysis committee composed of teachers on each grade along with reading and math specialists to match student responses on standardized tests with classroom instructional objectives and materials. There might be a disconnect with the textbooks and/or instructional materials used in reading and mathematics with the categories and types of test questions.

(3) These strategies might be effective in resolving these issues because matching teaching and learning with assessments will result in improved learning outcomes. Teachers would get a better handle on understanding their children's needs and would develop more appropriate differentiated learning activities.

Case 3

In conducting classroom observations, a high school principal notes that most of his teachers rely heavily on lecture as a method of instruction. After consulting with the district's administration, including the professional development coordinator, the principal secures funding for a two-day workshop on cooperative learning. The workshop takes place and all the teachers are enthusiastic about it. In the next cycle of faculty observations three months after the professional development program, the principal sees the same reliance on lecture as previously noted.

Directions:

Read the case carefully, and respond using scenario 2: (1) what did the administrator do well, (2) what did the administrator do poorly, (3) three actions the administrator might take to resolve the problem, and (4) why each action is likely to be effective.

Response:

(1) The principal recognized that instruction relies heavily on lecture. In looking at the achievement data, the principal found that achievement was negatively affected in those classes in which the teachers lectured. As a further support, the principal approached the district administration and secured funding for a two-day workshop on cooperative learning to address this issue.

(2) The principal neither assessed the needs of the teachers nor included them in the planning process for professional development. By imposing a professional development program, teachers had no stake in change.

(3) Three actions the principal might take to resolve the problem:
- Establish a School Achievement Committee, School Improvement Committee, or other governance committee consisting of teachers, administrators, and other stakeholders that is empowered to examine the data, look at possible teaching and learning models and make suggestions for change.
- Invite teacher buy-in by having on-going meetings with departments about appropriate instructional methodologies that might change their current instructional practices.
- Set up visitations to other high schools or inter-visitations within the high school to observe differentiated instruction, cooperative learning, and other teaching strategies so that staff might see their effect on teaching and learning.

6

(4)   These actions might be effective because it would provide for staff buy-in so that the change could take place. Deal and Peterson assert that change is most effective if participants have a stake in the change process. In giving teachers a host of best practices, they could internalize change with less resistance.

District based case studies:

Case 4

You are the Assistant Superintendent of Curriculum and Instruction of a middle class school district and chair a district committee for language arts. The committee includes an elementary, middle, and high school principal, an elementary, middle and high school "language arts" teacher, an elementary, middle, and high school parent, the teachers' union president, an elementary, middle and high school support staff member, a reading teacher from elementary, middle and high school, and a Board of Education member. The committee agreed to discuss strategies for improving reading throughout the grades. You presented a comprehensive plan that included the responsibilities of each staff member for improving reading at his/her respective grade. You also indicated the number of instructional periods for reading instruction at each grade level. From the outline you presented, it was clear that elementary school teachers spend significantly more time teaching reading than middle or high school teachers. At the next committee meeting, a parent member stated that the teachers in the middle and high school did not spend as much time teaching reading as the elementary school teachers. The parent asked, "Why is that taking place, if they make equivalent salaries?" The board member was listening intently to your response.

Directions:

Read the case carefully, and respond using scenario 1: (1) establish one strength of the administrator, (2) give one strategy for building on this strength, (3) indicate one weakness of the administrator, (4) give a strategy for addressing that weakness, and (5) knowing this information, why might these strategies be effective in resolving the case?

Response:

(1) The Assistant Superintendent was inclusive in establishing the membership of the district committee for language arts. As stated in the case, the committee includes elementary, middle and high school principals, secondary English language arts teachers, parents, the teachers' union president, support staff members, reading teachers, and a Board of Education member. Additionally, the Assistant Superintendent has obtained input from staff before presenting his/her report on reading to the committee.

(2) A strategy that the Assistant Superintendent might employ to build on being inclusive is to make sure that the Assistant Superintendent listens to all constituencies at committee meetings. This validates committee members as valued participants in the committee process. The Assistant Superintendent might establish subcommittees to examine critical issues with regard to reading at different instructional levels; e.g. instructional time for reading.

(3) A weakness of this case is that the Assistant Superintendent should have proactively discussed with the committee the differences in time for reading instruction at each level. The Assistant Superintendent should have been prepared with schedules, courses and graduation requirements so that discussion about reading instruction was supported by facts. Then the committee could make decisions that were well informed.

(4) A strategy for addressing this weakness is that the Assistant Superintendent should meet with each constituency to discuss the amount of time allocated for reading instruction at each level and suggest possible avenues for discussion at a full committee meeting. Likewise, by establishing sub-committees to look at reading issues at each instructional level, the Assistant Superintendent is sharing responsibilities for informed decision making. The Assistant Superintendent should have anticipated questions and prepared answers that would inform committee members.

(5) If the Assistant Superintendent puts all of these possibilities into play, then minimal resistance will occur at committee meetings.

Case 5

Dr. David Davis is the Director of Athletics of a suburban school district located within a middle class working community. As part of his job responsibilities, he supervises a number of coaches and assistant coaches who are in charge of a variety of sports teams at the high school and middle school. A Board of Education member saw Dr. Davis on the football field before last week's game and told Dr. Davis that his son did not get enough playing time. He wanted to know why this happened since his son had been to every practice and really wanted to play. Dr. Davis indicated that he would look into this matter and would get back to him. In discussing this issue with the head football coach and his assistants, Dr. Davis listened intently and was told that the youngster was obnoxious and did not listen to any of the coaches' directions during practices. In fact, the assistant coaches reported that they caught him breaking practice rules by sneaking out to have a snack during practice while texting his friends. Dr. Davis asked why this has not brought to his attention earlier and they indicated that they were hesitant because he was the son of a board member. Dr. Davis set up a meeting with the Board of Education member regarding this matter.

Directions:

Read the case carefully, and respond using scenario 2: (1) what did the administrator do well, (2) what did the administrator do poorly, (3) what three actions might the administrator take to resolve the problem, and (4) why is each action is likely to be effective.

Response:

(1) Before making any snap decisions, Dr. Davis asked the coaches what was going on with regard to this particular youngster's participation. Dr. Davis was a good listener and treated conversations with the coaching staff as highly important in the decision making process. Likewise, Dr. Davis did not dismiss the board member's concern, but offered to discuss the issue further after he looked into the matter.

(2) The Athletic Director should have shared the problem with the Superintendent since there might be some political implication. Additionally, Dr. Davis should have asked the coaches to interview and provide statements from other members of the football team to corroborate the observed behaviors of the school board member's son.

(3) Three actions the Athletic Director should take to resolve the problem:

- Meet with the Superintendent to explain the issue and get input.
- Meet with all coaches to instruct them to regularly share extraordinary situations that might affect sports programs at regular coaching meetings. At such meetings the Athletic Director should discuss the possibility of having rules of participation written and signed by all student athletes and their parents.
- Set up a meeting with the Board of Education member, the head football coach and himself to explain why the board member's son was less than honest with his father about his commitment to the football program. In order to retain the youngster in the football program, it might be necessary to develop a written contract with the student.

(4) Effective communication, both written and verbal, can head off issues that might arise between parents, coaches and students even if the parent is a Board of Education member.

Case 6

The Superintendent of an affluent suburban school district comprised of five elementary schools, two middle schools, and one high school was disturbed over the weekend by an incident that took place in the community. The incident involved a high school girl who was arrested by the police for driving under the influence. Upon questioning, she told the police that she was smoking marijuana while at a party. When asked where she purchased the marijuana, the girl told the police that marijuana was readily available at the high school and that she purchased the marijuana from another girl in the cafeteria. Immediately upon hearing this, the police captain called the Superintendent, indicating that the police wanted to search the building with dogs as soon as possible during the school day. To complicate matters, a Board of Education member approached the Superintendent shortly after the incident occurred and demanded an immediate course of action in response to the youngster's arrest. The Superintendent told the board member that his administrative team would present a substance abuse and prevention plan for the high school at next month's Board of Education meeting. The Superintendent also informed the police that he would arrange an immediate meeting with the high school administration to implement a timely school wide search for marijuana with the least amount of disruption to the school day.

Directions:

Read the case carefully, and respond using scenario 3: (1) identify two key issues in the case, (2) give one strategy you might employ to resolve each issue identified, and (3) explain how that strategy might be effective in resolving the issues.

Response:

(1) Two key issues in this case are:
- A high school girl was arrested by the police for driving under the influence. She indicated she purchased the marijuana in school, as it was readily available there.
- A Board of Education member is demanding an immediate plan of action in response to the girl being arrested off campus for using marijuana.
- The police want to search the school for marijuana using dogs during the school day.

(2) A strategy that the Superintendent might employ to resolve each issue is multi-pronged. The Superintendent should involve the high school

principal and the high school administrative staff in developing an immediate short-term plan that includes working with the police and school attorney regarding search and seizure of drugs at the high school. Furthermore, the administrative team should develop an action plan involving staff, the parent organization, students, and the police regarding the existence of a possible substance abuse problem at the high school. Additionally, the Superintendent should establish a district substance abuse committee. The committee should include the representation from high school teaching staff and administration, the Director of Health, a high school parent, a local police officer (youth bureau), the school district physician, a high school student, and the Superintendent to develop a long-range action plan for the school district regarding substance abuse. Because the Board of Education member approached the Superintendent seeking immediate action, the Superintendent should inform the board member that a plan is in the process of development by a broad based constituency, which would be shared with the Board of Education at the next meeting indicating next steps.

(3)   This strategy might be effective in resolving the issue because it involves a broad based constituency in addressing the sensitive issue of substance abuse at the high school. With a variety of constituents giving their input to the development of an action plan, it would be more likely to be effective and receive broad based support and funding necessary for successful implementation.

Chapter 2

Standard 2: *to promote the success of all students, promote a positive school culture, provide an effective instructional program, apply best practice to student learning, and design comprehensive professional growth plans for staff*

Chapter 2

Standard 2: *to promote the success of all students, promote a positive school culture, provide an effective instructional program, apply best practice to student learning, and design comprehensive professional growth plans for staff*

School based cases:

Case 7
Dr. Roberta Santiago is the assistant principal in charge of the world languages department. This year, one teacher must teach a sixth class, Spanish, where the collective bargaining agreement allows five classes per teacher, with a sixth class to incur extra compensation. One new untenured Spanish teacher would take the class if no one else volunteered to teach the sixth period. A tenured male Spanish teacher asked to teach the class, hoping to boost his final average salary before retirement. While the tenured teacher has evidenced solid performance over the years, Dr. Santiago believes that he would not do the best job with the additional class and the burden of having a sixth class would ultimately negatively affect his performance in other classes. Dr. Santiago believes the newer teacher would be better suited for the additional class and would have the stamina to perform well for the year. Dr. Santiago also knows that the newer teacher could use the money.

Directions:
Read the case carefully, and respond using scenario 1: (1) establish one strength of the administrator, (2) give one strategy for building on this strength, (3) indicate one weakness of the administrator, (4) give a strategy for addressing that weakness, and (5) knowing this information, why might these strategies be effective in resolving the case.

Response:
(1) Dr. Santiago knows the strengths and weaknesses of the world language staff. Additionally, she has the best interest of the students in mind if she assigns the sixth class to the newer Spanish language teacher.

(2) A strategy that the assistant principal might employ to support her decision is to meet individually with each teacher and discuss the possible additional responsibilities in teaching a sixth class to the teaching schedule. The assistant principal could point out to each teacher that the

additional load of the sixth class might be stressful and time consuming. Dr. Santiago should also confer with the building principal to secure support in the assignment of the newer teacher. The building principal might have additional suggestions as to how to proceed prior to making this assignment or might even want to intercede and meet with each candidate in a "mini-interview" to select the better-qualified teacher. The principal might also suggest that the assistant principal establish an interview committee prior to making the assignment so that the best candidate actually receives this additional responsibility.

(3) A weakness of the assistant principal might be her decision-making abilities. Confronted with a difficult decision, an administrator must accurately assess the alternatives and make a decision that benefits the instructional program. Making a difficult decision might be unpopular with staff but an effective rationale to support her decision making would be keeping the best interests of the students in mind at all times.

(4) Perhaps the assistant principal might build support for her decision by announcing that her decision would be based upon the educational needs of the school. Clearly, if the assistant principal articulated the qualifications for teaching the sixth class prior to selection of an appropriate teacher, the selection process would be transparent to administrators and teachers alike. Hopefully, those needs are more in alignment with the qualifications of the newer teacher.

(5) These strategies might be effective because we know that the more people are aware of the factors within the decision-making process, the greater the chances the decision will be supported.

Case 8

You are the principal of a middle school. In one of your regular walks around the building and in your casual conversations with teachers, you learn that one teacher, besides being a minute or two late most days, is not keeping up his responsibilities. You check his personnel file. In the file, you find letters reporting that he is never in the halls during passing, and when he is walking to the cafeteria or the bathroom and sees trouble, he looks the other way. Instructionally, prior observations have indicated that he frequently assigns independent deskwork to his students. Colleagues report to you that he frequently plays on his computer during class time (researching real estate, perusing the shopping websites, etc.). The assistant principal reports that he allows his students to do whatever they wish, including moving about the room to chat with friends. The department chair reports that he takes a newspaper to read during department meetings.

Directions:

Read the case carefully, and respond using scenario 2: (1) what did the administrator do well, (2) what did the administrator do poorly, (3) three actions the administrator might take to resolve the problem, and (4) why each action is likely to be effective.

Response:

(1) The principal is highly visible around the building, conversing with teachers while making "rounds." Apparently, the principal has the pulse of the building.

(2) The principal did not attack this issue earlier. This teacher has displayed aberrant behavior over time and apparently, neither the department chairperson nor the assistant principal/building principal has developed an intervention plan for this teacher.

(3) Three actions the principal might take:
- Regular visits to this teacher's classroom to observe teacher behavior and instructional competence.
- As inappropriate performance has been observed in/out of the classroom, letters to the teacher's file should have been regularly provided.
- Development of an intervention plan by the administrative team to improve performance should have been provided.

(4) Each one of the above actions might be effective because:

- Regular visits will give the principal a better opportunity to assess teaching performance and provide the teacher constructive feedback regarding teaching and learning.
- Letters of inappropriate performance will put the teacher on notice that his behavior is unacceptable and unsatisfactory. It should lead to an intervention program developed collaboratively with the teacher and principal.
- An intervention plan will outline acceptable behaviors and a path to achieve satisfactory performance and develop appropriate mechanisms to achieve this goal.

Case 9

You are the assistant principal in charge of after school programs and have been directed by the principal (who was directed by the Superintendent) to keep a record of after-school extra help, which you understand to mean that teachers must now keep logs of their extra-help classes and a roster of who attends. You know that the teachers will see this as additional unnecessary paperwork under the guise of greater "accountability." You know that keeping such records, let alone handing them in, is against past practices in this building but you are not privy to any action you suspect the teachers' association might take in this regard. You need to abide by the directive and to make the whole thing work.

Directions:

Read the case carefully, and respond using scenario 3: (1) identify two key issues in the case, (2) give one strategy you might employ to resolve each issue identified, and (3) explain how that strategy might be effective in resolving the issues.

Response:

(1) Key issues in this case are:

- Implementing an accountability program for teachers working in an after school extra help program where none had existed.
- Teachers complain of the additional paperwork.
- Actions the teachers' association might take regarding this new initiative.

(2) A strategy the assistant principal might employ to resolve each of these issues:

- Set up a meeting with teachers working in the after school program and ask them to help provide a solution to an issue that needs resolution. By sharing the responsibility of identifying the problem, the teachers' suggestions become more important in resolving the record keeping issue.
- Establish a committee of teachers working in the program to examine how they could establish the needed accountability with a minimum of paperwork.
- Meet with the president of the teachers' association when the problem presented itself and ask for input. Perhaps the teachers' association might become a willing participant in resolving the accountability issue so that teachers do not have negative feelings about participating in after school programs.

(3) Decisions are most effective if participants share in the decision making process. With teachers and teachers' association participation in developing mechanisms for accountability, the chance of developing a negative reaction to the resolution has been reduced. Working together, the assistant principal and teachers can satisfactorily resolve this issue.

District based cases:

Case 10

Dr. Beatrice Harris is the Superintendent of a large metropolitan school district with over 8,000 children housed in eight elementary schools, four middle schools, and two high schools. The children come from a variety of ethnic backgrounds, with 55% of the population Caucasian and the balance of the population equally split between Latino and African American students. There is a wide range of income levels residing in the district, from upper middle class to poverty level students and their families. Dr. Harris was hired a year ago on a platform of addressing the achievement gap for minority children. The Board of Education has five members: four non-minority members, and one minority member. The board wants immediate action to address the minority achievement gap. As Dr. Harris makes regular visits around the school district and talks with administrators and teachers, she is astounded with teacher negativism regarding minority achievement. Dr. Harris shared with principals what she heard from teachers during a principals' meeting and asked for their recommendations. All but two of the principals made recommendations that supported the teachers' negativism. Dr. Harris asked the two principals that agreed with her to see her after the meeting. She asked, "Why is everyone so negative?" The principals related a story about the previous Superintendent who had required teachers to implement a new initiative every year. Although reducing the minority achievement gap was extremely important, the principals felt that the other administrators have been jaded because undertaking another new initiative, especially one that the staff has not enthusiastically supported, would be foolish.

Directions:

Read the case carefully, and respond using scenario 1: (1) establish one strength of the administrator, (2) give one strategy for building on this strength, (3) indicate one weakness of the administrator, (4) give a strategy for addressing that weakness, and (5) knowing this information, why might these strategies be effective in resolving the case.

Response:

(1) A strength of the Superintendent was that she was willing to discuss the issue of the minority achievement gap with her principals and get their input. Dr. Harris was clearly visible around the district, regularly visiting the schools, greeting teachers and listening to what they have to say.

(2) A strategy the Superintendent could employ is to establish a working committee with principals, teachers, and parents to study the issue of reducing the minority achievement gap, set long term and short-term goals with regard to reducing the achievement gap and communicate those goals to all constituencies.

(3) A weakness of the Superintendent was that she assured the Board of Education that immediate action was forthcoming before meeting with the principals or establishing a committee to address this issue. The Superintendent wanted to appear decisive in reassuring the Board of Education but giving the Board of Education a commitment before sizing up the breadth and scope of the issue is troublesome. Additionally, the Superintendent should have interviewed other administrators and teachers to gather their prospective regarding the issue.

(4) The Superintendent should meet with Board of Education members to address her hasty commitment to action. She should acknowledge that the achievement gap must be addressed and give each board member a reassurance that a plan and timeline for change is being developed, which will have broad based support from a variety of constituencies because their participation in the change process is crucial.

(5) By involving the Board of Education members and a variety of constituencies in the change process, addressing the achievement gap will not become another "one and done" program, but it will change the cultural expectations of teachers and administrators.

Case 11

Dr. Victoria Casey is the Assistant Superintendent for Curriculum and Instruction in a suburban school district with the responsibility of enacting a comprehensive professional development plan. In her visits to schools and discussion with school-based administrators, they suggest to her that she concentrate on reading and writing. Dr. Casey then developed a professional development plan for improving reading and writing instruction across the grades, and brought it before the Board of Education for ratification at a public meeting. The Board of Education asked for public comment about the plan. The president of the teachers' association stood up and voiced his disapproval of the plan. Likewise, the president of the district-wide parents' council also stood up and disapproved of the plan. The Board of Education president turned towards Dr. Casey and asked for an explanation. Subsequently the board tabled the motion for ratification of the plan.

Directions:

Read the case carefully, and respond using scenario 2: (1) what did the administrator do well, (2) what did the administrator do poorly, (3) what are three actions the administrator might take to resolve the problem, and (4) why is each action is likely to be effective.

Response:

(1) The Assistant Superintendent, Dr. Casey, sought input from the district's administrative staff. The Assistant Superintendent brought the plan before the Board of Education for ratification.

(2) The Assistant Superintendent did not consult with other constituencies, including the Superintendent, teachers and parents, before developing the plan. Additionally, she did not share the plan with the Superintendent before it was presented to the Board of Education.

(3) Three actions the Assistant Superintendent could take to resolve the problem:

- Withdraw the current plan from ratification, establish a professional development committee with representatives of all constituencies, including teachers, administrators, parents, and other staff and develop a comprehensive professional development plan.
- Consult with the Superintendent about the process before sending the plan to the Board of Education.

- Distribute a district wide needs assessment regarding comprehensive professional development needs.

(4) By bringing all constituencies to the table to review concerns over professional development, the plan developed would then have broad based support for Board of Education approval.

Case 12

The Assistant Superintendent for Curriculum and Instruction received the district's annual achievement scores from the State Education Department. After reviewing them and compiling a summary, the Assistant Superintendent forwarded the materials and the analysis to the Superintendent for review and dissemination. Upon carefully perusing the analysis the Assistant Superintendent prepared, the Superintendent saw that reading achievement scores dipped on average five percent below the previous year's scores in one of the district elementary schools. The Superintendent was concerned and called the principal of that school to the central office to discuss this issue with the Superintendent and staff. At the meeting, the Superintendent expressed disappointment with the principal's instructional leadership and shared an intervention plan developed by the Assistant Superintendent specifically for improving reading achievement at the elementary school. The Superintendent wanted the plan implemented immediately.

Directions:

Read the case carefully, and respond using scenario 3: (1) identify two key issues in the case, (2) give one strategy you might employ to resolve each issue identified, and (3) explain how that strategy might be effective in resolving the issues.

Response:

(1) Two key issues are:

- The Assistant Superintendent developed an improvement plan without input from a variety of stakeholders at the elementary school including the building principal, teachers, support staff, and related service providers who could provide insight toward developing a meaningful intervention program.
- By the Superintendent expressing disappointment with the school's reading scores and the principal's lack of instructional leadership, the Superintendent created an adversarial relationship and an atmosphere of distrust and ill will that would be transferred back to the school.

(2) A strategy that the principal might employ to resolve this issue is to request that the Superintendent give the principal an opportunity to review the scores with a school committee and develop a school-based improvement plan that would have the "buy-in" of the various constituencies. The principal could come back to the Superintendent with

a school-developed plan based upon data analyzed at the school level by the committee.

(3) By developing a localized plan with a variety of constituents involved in the planning process, the probability for success is greater.

Chapter 3

Standard 3: *to ensure management of the organization, operations, and resources for a safe, efficient, and effective learning environment*

Chapter 3

Standard 3: *to ensure management of the organization, operations, and resources for a safe, efficient, and effective learning environment*

School based case studies:

Case 13

Mr. Sam Silver is the assistant principal in charge of discipline at a middle school. One morning the dean told him that a boy found a "hit list" on his desk naming him and four other boys. The "reporting" boy, "Rudolph," was known to have difficulty making friends and would do just about anything to get attention. Mr. Silver interviewed Rudolph and suspected that Rudolph wrote and titled the list himself. Mr. Silver checked the handwriting on the note with Rudolph. He found that Rudolph wrote his own name in his own unique style, drawing a smiley face on the letter "R" on both the note and in his notebook. Mr. Silver and the dean questioned Rudolph who vehemently denied that he wrote the "hit list." He provided the assistant principal a written statement in which he claimed not to know who might be responsible. Mr. Silver continued to investigate the incident by interviewing the other boys named on the list, getting their statements, and informing their parents of the situation. None of them claims to have any enemies and none was able to guess who would have put their names on a "hit list." Mr. Silver concluded that Rudolph wrote the hit list. As a matter of procedure, Mr. Silver called Rudolph's mother; she could not believe that he accused her son of writing a "hit list." She threatened a lawsuit against the district for causing her son anxiety and damaging his reputation. Mr. Silver informed the principal who suspended Rudolph. Meanwhile, word has gotten out that there *was* a "hit list" and that a number of students have been named on it. Mr. Silver received ten phone calls from "concerned parents" about impending violence at the Middle School.

Directions:

Read the case carefully, and respond using scenario 1: (1) establish one strength of the administrator, (2) give one strategy for building on this strength, (3) indicate one weakness of the administrator, (4) give a strategy for addressing that weakness, and (5) knowing this information, why might these strategies be effective in resolving the case.

Response:

(1) Mr. Silver supported the dean's initial investigation of the incident. The assistant principal further investigated the incident, interviewing students that might have been associated with the situation, before coming to a decision on guilt.

(2) The assistant principal did not accuse Rudolph without examining the evidence and obtaining statements from Rudolph and the other students. A thorough investigation would involve looking at a variety of evidence, both verbal and written, to accurately assess who might have been the guilty party before making any decision.

(3) The assistant principal should have discussed the incident with the principal after completing his interviews so that the principal would have been involved in the disciplinary procedure earlier, especially one that would have school wide implications. The principal, in turn, could have contacted the Superintendent and the district's legal counsel so that appropriate legal advice was available to the building administrative staff and a more informed decision could have been made regarding Rudolph's guilt.

(4) The assistant principal and principal meet with the Superintendent as soon as possible to share the evidence and discuss possible disciplinary actions against Rudolph and implications for the school community since the rumor mill has started. The assistant principal should also call the parents of the students on the "hit list" reassuring them that appropriate action has been taken to ensure the safety of their children. After the meeting, upon direction from the principal, the assistant principal should involve the police. Moreover, with regard to the rumor mill, the principal should be proactive and use the school's phone messenger system to communicate with parents.

(5) These strategies might be effective in resolving the case because all parties have become aware of the incident, having seen and discussed the evidence, and been involved in the decision making process. Communication is crucial to avert crises. Moreover, decisions are supported more often when stakeholders share involvement in the process.

Case 14

Finances may be the catch-22 of administration. As principal of a large high school, you must manage them, and manage them wisely, even though you have little control over the amounts of money that are allocated for specific expenditures. This year the Superintendent and Assistant Superintendent for Business informed you that there is money available for one, and only one, big expenditure at your school. You have been asked to make the decision either to replace all the old hallway lockers or to install interactive Smart boards in all the remaining classrooms without them. The Assistant Superintendent for Business wants an immediate response. You convene a cabinet meeting of the high school administrators to discuss this pending expenditure before responding to the Assistant Superintendent for Business.

Directions:

Read the case carefully, and respond using scenario 2: (1) what did the administrator do well, (2) what did the administrator do poorly, (3) three actions the administrator might take to resolve the problem, and (4) why each action is likely to be effective.

Response:

(1) Although the Assistant Superintendent wanted an immediate response, the principal convened a cabinet meeting so that at least the administrative staff might have some input into this issue: lockers vs. Smartboards.

(2) The principal should have surveyed the school based governance council, shared decision-making team or staff to seek their input. Time permitting, the principal could disseminate a need assessment to get input.

(3) Three actions the principal might take in order to make a decision with a majority buy-in:
- The principal might consult with a variety of constituencies within the school to get a decision with broad based support. Teachers, parents and students might be consulted for their input to prioritize the upcoming expenditure.
- The principal could meet with the Assistant Superintendent for Business to see if there is any flexibility in the use of these funds or perhaps if the principal could re-direct other funds in the school's budget to support more than one initiative.

- The principal could seek outside funding sources to support one of the initiatives not funded, e.g. Parent Organization or local business support for Smartboards.

(4) Decision making with a broad consensus is the most effective.

Case 15
You are the assistant principal of a large middle school. The chief custodian has been complaining to you loudly and clearly that the graffiti in the boys' bathrooms in your area of the building is getting worse (in frequency of occurrence, in extent of damage, and in disgusting expressions). The tactics you have taken in the past, e.g. closing the bathrooms for repair sometimes for days, calling for class sign-out sheets, stationing duty teachers in the halls when available and questioning students reported to be suspicious have neither helped to resolve the chief custodian's ire nor resolved the problem.

Directions:
Read the case carefully, and respond using scenario 3: (1) identify two key issues in the case, (2) give one strategy you might employ to resolve each issue identified, and (3) explain how that strategy might be effective in resolving the issues.

Response:
(1) Two key issues in this case:
- Boys are abusing the use of the boys' bathrooms by producing excessive graffiti and physically abusing the facility.
- The chief custodian is irate with the condition of the boys' bathrooms.

(2) A strategy that the assistant principal might employ to resolve this issue:
- Send a letter or email to parents of boys indicating that some of the boys' bathrooms have recently been marked with graffiti. Ask for the parents' cooperation and support in speaking with their boys about respectfully using these facilities. Additionally, the assistant principal should speak with all the boys to encourage appropriate decorum when using the bathroom. The assistant principal could also set up a committee to upgrade the boys' bathrooms; what could the school do to make the rooms' user friendly. Furthermore, the assistant principal should discuss the problem with teachers (especially on that particular side of the building) for input of possible alternatives that might reduce the abuse of the boys' bathrooms.
- The assistant principal should meet with the chief custodian to discuss the steps taken regarding solving the problem. The assistant principal should point out that the school must ensure the

cleanliness of the boys' bathroom even with increasing graffiti. Dirty bathrooms invite trouble; the nicer they look, the longer they go untouched. Ask the chief custodian if he has any insights into ways the school might resolve this problem.

(3) This strategy might be effective in resolving the problem by creating a climate of respect for use of the boys' bathrooms, while at the same time involving students, parents, and staff to assure their cleanliness.

District based case studies:

Case 16

Dr. Frank Regal is the Assistant Superintendent for Business of a suburban school district, with seven elementary schools, two middle schools, and one high school. The Superintendent has asked Dr. Regal to prepare a mid-year budget report for the Board of Education. The report indicated a projected deficit of $1.0 million. The Superintendent requested that Dr. Regal provide him with projected spending cuts to bring the budget into alignment. Dr. Regal returned to his office and worked tirelessly over the next four hours to provide budget reduction recommendations to the Superintendent of $1.0 million. In his work, he attempted to reduce spending throughout the budgets of all the schools, as well as looking at general district-wide expenditures. After reviewing the proposed budget reductions, the Superintendent told Dr. Regal to enact the plan immediately.

Directions:

Read the case carefully, and respond using scenario 1: (1) identify one strength of the administrator, (2) give one strategy for building on this strength, (3) indicate one weakness of the administrator, (4)give a strategy for addressing that weakness, and (5) knowing this information, why might these strategies be effective in resolving the case.

Response:

(1)   Dr. Regal, Assistant Superintendent for Business, identified the potential for having a significant fiscal problem with an impending deficit of $1.0 million and immediately made recommendations to remedy the problem.

(2)   After recognizing that the budget was out of alignment, Dr. Regal should have issued a written communication to district and school based administrative staff requesting a meeting to discuss budget-cutting alternatives. At that meeting, the Assistant Superintendent should have led a discussion about the core values and programs that were "sacred cows" that define the district. In this way, ownership of the problem would not be restricted only to the business officer but rather inclusive of all district financial responsibility centers.

(3)   A weakness of the Assistant Superintendent for Business is that he was working in a vacuum to address the deficit.

(4) He should have prepared a report indicating areas for proposed budget reductions and then met with administrators so that they could jointly recommend to the Superintendent appropriate budget reductions. This plan would have broad based support across district financial responsibility centers. This inclusive approach to budget reductions makes all constituencies involved take ownership in the process.

(5) These strategies might be effective because by involving a broad based group of administrators in the decision making process, the potential negativism about the budget reduction might be reduced since all parties have had an opportunity to be part of the solution.

Case 17

Dr. Rita Mellon is the Superintendent of a small suburban school district that has two elementary schools, one middle school and one high school. In touring the facilities with the Director of Buildings and Grounds over the summer to observe the interior and exterior condition of the buildings, Dr. Mellon pointed out that the flower beds adjacent to the school buildings were filled with debris, weeds, and were unsightly. Dr. Mellon wanted the flowerbeds attended to before school opened in September and covered with fresh mulch. The buildings and grounds landscape crew consisted of five workers, two of whom had requested and already scheduled vacations during the upcoming weeks over the summer. The Director of Buildings and Grounds informed Dr. Mellon that he could not get his reduced workforce to work any harder and, with their vacations set, they could not take on any additional work. Dr. Mellon was not pleased with the director's statement. Dr. Mellon ordered the director and his landscape crew to meet with her the next morning.

Directions:

Read the case carefully, and respond using scenario 2: (1) what did the administrator do well, (2) what did the administrator do poorly, (3) three actions the administrator might take to resolve the problem, and (4) why is each action likely to be effective.

Response:

(1) The Superintendent, Dr. Mellon, toured the facilities with the Director of Buildings and Grounds to observe the interior and exterior condition of the buildings and grounds to see if they were ready for the upcoming school year. Although it appears to be an issue of micromanagement, the big picture of getting the buildings ready for the upcoming school year is commendable.

(2) Dr. Mellon should not take over the management of buildings and grounds but should work with the director in developing a plan that would comply with her timeframe for beautifying the grounds.

(3) Three actions the Superintendent should take to resolve the problem:
- Let the Director of Buildings and Grounds and his landscape crew develop a workable timeframe so that all exterior work could be completed before school starts.
- Request the Director of Buildings and Grounds provide the Superintendent with regular updates of interior and exterior

maintenance so that additional personnel might be shifted to assist the maintenance crew in completing the task.

- Ask the director if additional summer help and/or additional overtime would resolve the issue of staffing over the summer months. Perhaps a small expenditure of funds for overtime hours might prove to be an effective incentive to get the job done. Additionally, by hiring additional hourly employees or student workers, the summer crunch for completion of interior and exterior maintenance might ease.

(4)   If the Superintendent involved herself in the workings of every department, that department would become less effective in completing required tasks in a timely basis.   In addition, her own time would be rapidly depleted.   Dr. Mellon must learn to trust and support the administrators she hired to run their departments effectively and efficiently.

Case 18

Dr. John Simon was selected as the Superintendent of a small suburban school district, having one early childhood center, two elementary schools, one middle school, and one high school. In order to develop a better relationship with the Board of Education, Dr. Simon requested that Board of Education members join him on a weekend retreat at a regional conference center. The conference center provided a large meeting room, three buffet meals per day, and lodging for two nights for the Superintendent, two Assistant Superintendents, and five Board of Education members. The conference center was located at the shore with all rooms having a fantastic view of the water. Additionally, the facility included a business center, health center, and day spa. Dr. Simon conducted a successful retreat with board members. The Superintendent signed the bill for payment, which included a liquor bill and spa treatments for Board of Education members. When the Assistant Superintendent for Business reviewed the retreat bill for payment, he noticed that there was a liquor charge and a charge for spa treatments for board members. The Assistant Superintendent for Business told Dr. Simon that those expenditures were not in alignment with state spending guidelines for conferences.

Directions:

Read the case carefully, and respond using scenario 3: (1) identify two key issues in the case, (2) give one strategy you might employ to resolve each issue identified, and (3) explain how that strategy might be effective in resolving the issues.

Response:

(1) Two key issues:

- The Superintendent, Dr. Simon, conducted a weekend retreat with staff and Board of Education members, whose costs were not authorized according to state guidelines for allowable expenses at conferences.
- At the conclusion of the retreat, the Superintendent signed the bill accepting charges for liquor and spa treatments. Since the Superintendent signed the billed, he was personally liable for those expenditures. If a claim for reimbursement was made by the Superintendent, those expenditures should be deducted from the claim.

(2) Both issues deal with fiscal improprieties, namely having liquor and spa treatments at an official event paid for with public funds. There are two possible roads the Superintendent might take to resolve this issue. Firstly, he could send a memo to board members requesting they reimburse the district for liquor they consumed and spa treatments they took. Secondly, the Superintendent could pay for those items he authorized as a personal expenditure.

(3) By removing the unauthorized expenditures for reimbursement, it would take away any cloud of impropriety regarding misuse of public funds that could overhang the retreat. In receiving reimbursement for claims of that nature, the Superintendent is risking high-level consequences for fiscal impropriety. Prior to taking their seats on the Board of Education, all board members were instructed on fiscal improprieties and their consequences.

Chapter 4

Standard 4*: to collaborate with families and community members, to respond to diverse community interests and needs, and to mobilize community resources*

Chapter 4

Standard 4: *to collaborate with families and community members, to respond to diverse community interests and needs, and to mobilize community resources*

School based case studies:

Case 19

Mrs. Rita Jones is the assistant principal of a middle school in charge of assembly programs. She works very closely with the school based Cultural Arts Committee and Parent Organization to select programs that advance the character education program, inform, and entertain the students. However, at midyear, a number of core teachers complained that their students were pulled out of the same classes too often for assembly programs that they could do without. Moreover, teachers informed Mrs. Jones that some assembly programs did not address students' needs. Mrs. Jones has a dilemma: what should she do, both in terms of the assembly schedule remaining this year and in scheduling assemblies next year?

Directions:

Read the case carefully, and respond using scenario 1: (1) establish one strength of the administrator, (2) give one strategy for building on this strength, (3) indicate one weakness of the administrator, (4) give a strategy for addressing that weakness, and (5) knowing this information, why might these strategies be effective in resolving the case.

Response:

(1) The assistant principal recognized the importance of infusing cultural arts and character education into the curriculum. She validated the work of the Cultural Arts Committee and Parent Organization by scheduling a variety of assembly programs throughout the school year.

(2) A strategy for building on this strength might be to disseminate a survey to staff and students after each assembly program to assess the program's effectiveness in attaining the committee's goal. Survey results could be shared with the committee and Parent Organization to address issues resulting from implementing the assembly program. Additionally, Mrs. Jones should develop a needs assessment for dissemination to staff regarding programming for the next school year.

(3) Mrs. Jones' weakness is that programs developed by the cultural arts committee and Parent Organization did not receive support from the teaching staff. Additionally, scheduling cultural arts programs interfered with core class instructional time; teachers felt that loss of instructional time was significant.

(4) A strategy for addressing that weakness might include meeting with the cultural arts committee and Parent Organization to consider scheduling assemblies at different times during the school day so that loss of instructional time be minimized. Additionally, assembly programs need to be integrated into the core instructional program with activities that might be reinforced in core classrooms. Furthermore, by conducting a needs assessment with core teachers, assembly programs could be more aligned with instruction.

(5) Win-win solutions are important to support the instructional program. We know that character education is a vital component of a middle school instructional program; at the same time, loss of instructional time is an on-going complaint of core teachers. By providing opportunities to integrate special programs into daily instruction with input from core teachers and rotating presentation time of those programs, teachers' complaints have been addressed.

Case 20

Dr. James Angelo is an elementary school principal of a K – 5 school with a population of 435 students located within a middle class community of a moderate sized city. The school is surrounded by modest homes. The school built in the 1960's, has an expansive classroom space on one level and an extensive playground, a blacktop area, and a rather large grass field. Dr. Angelo developed a good relationship with his neighbors; they watch the property on weekends so that graffiti and improper use of grounds has been minimal over the years. A homeowner whose property is adjacent to the school called Dr. Angelo to complain that the children were making too much noise during recess. The neighbor said that the noise was disturbing her elderly mother who was not well. Dr. Angelo was curt and told his neighbor that there is nothing he could do, reinforcing that the neighbor lives next to a school and children do make some noise during recess.

Directions:

Read the case carefully, and respond using scenario 2: (1) what did the administrator do well, (2) what did the administrator do poorly, (3) three actions the administrator might take to resolve the problem, and (4) why each action is likely to be effective.

Response:

(1) The principal has established a good relationship with his neighbors; neighbors keep an eye on the school building and grounds when school is not in session.

(2) The principal should not have brushed off his neighbor, thereby creating ill will amongst community members living adjacent to the school.

(3) Three actions the principal might take:
- In meeting with the neighbor, the principal could ascertain when during recess was the noise an issue and consider shifting the outdoor recess to other areas in the field that hopefully would minimize the elderly person's discomfort. In addition, he could remind the neighbor that during the winter month's outdoor recess was constrained by the weather.
- Invite the neighbor to meet with the school planning committee to share her concerns about noise during recess.

- Create a program recognizing the efforts of community members in support of school activities and security.

(4) Each action would be effective in building a lasting relationship with community members.

Case 21

You are the principal of a K – 6 school. It is a tradition that all sixth grade classes participate in an overnight camping experience at a local environmental education center. Each sixth grade class has two parent chaperones assigned to the class for the overnight trip. Chaperones were selected from a pool of parent volunteers who signed an agreement to abide by the school rules for overnight trips. The rules were previously shared with parents. Every chaperone has a cell phone whose number is registered with the school. When they arrived at the environmental education center, the teachers assigned parent chaperones to each class to help get the children settled at their campsite. All went well and the children were settled for the night. However, you receive a frantic telephone call at home at 11:30 P.M. from a teacher on the trip that a parent chaperone was reported by another parent to be drinking in a bar after the children went to sleep.

Directions:

Read the case carefully, and respond using scenario 3: (1) identify two key issues in the case, (2) give one strategy you might employ to resolve each issue identified, and (3) explain how that strategy might be effective in resolving the issues.

Response:

(1) Two key issues in this case include:

- A chaperone was reported by another parent to be drinking during the overnight camping trip in violation of the code of conduct for chaperones.
- The principal was unable to make an informed decision as to the accuracy of the incident because neither he nor the sixth grade teacher witnessed what the parent reported.

(2) A strategy that the principal might employ to resolve the first issue is call the chaperone that was thought to be drinking on his/her cell phone and ask if the allegation is true. The principal should remind the chaperone of the agreement the chaperone signed prior to the trip which indicated that inappropriate behavior, such as drinking in a bar, would have consequences. After hearing the response of the chaperone, the principal could order the chaperone to return home immediately. A second strategy that the principal might employ is appointing a teacher as a "teacher-in-charge" prior to departure so that all participants know and understand that the teacher-in-charge has the power of the principal in his

absence. The "teacher-in-charge" could then take statements from all chaperones as to where they were after the children went to sleep. The teacher-in-charge could also check with the bar to confirm that the parent was present and then send the chaperone home.

(3) These strategies might be effective in resolving this incident because if chaperones knew that someone was serving as a trip supervisor with the power of the principal, expectations for aberrant behavior might be diminished. Additionally, the teacher-in-charge could reinforce with chaperones "face-to-face" that after the children went to bed leaving the camp grounds would be a violation of the agreement that chaperones signed before they left for the overnight camping experience.

District based case studies:

Case 22
Dr. Thomas Kelly is the Superintendent of a suburban school district with changing demographics. When he was hired, the district had 3000 children attending public schools and 2800 children attending private religious schools, with the Board of Education members primarily parents of public school children. Three years later, there are 3000 children attending private schools and 2800 children attend the public schools, with the Board of Education members primarily parents of private school children. Dr. Kelly indicated to the Board of Education and community that he is ready, willing, and able to work with all groups in the community for the education of all children. It is clear that the public school community cannot gather enough support to elect public school parents to the Board of Education because of the changing demographics. The parents of public school children feel disenfranchised and believe that resources are not being equitably distributed. They feel that their children are being shortchanged. Public school parents are hostile at every Board of Education meeting, constantly questioning every action Dr. Kelly proposes, and each resolution the Board of Education approves.

Directions:
Read the case carefully, and respond using scenario 1: (1) establish one strength of the administrator, (2) give one strategy for building on this strength, (3) indicate one weakness of the administrator, (4) give a strategy for addressing that weakness, and (5) knowing this information, Why might these strategies be effective in resolving the case?

Response:
(1) The Superintendent has publicly expressed that he is ready, willing, and able to work with all members of the community for the education of all children.

(2) The Superintendent should seek out leaders from both the public and non-public school communities and meet with them regularly to discuss common issues affecting the education of children in both communities. He could then establish an agenda for addressing common problems. Additionally, Dr. Kelly must re-establish trust in the function of the school district for the public school community. Likewise, the non-public school community must be recognized by the public school parents as a force in the community affecting the budgetary process. Clearly define what can

and cannot be supported with public funds so that all constituencies are clear about this issue.

(3) One weakness is the situation that the Superintendent finds himself in; he must respond to a non-public dominated Board of Education whose membership does not understand the workings of a public school system.

(4) A strategy for addressing this issue is to assign Board of Education members to serve as liaisons to each public school, asking them to regularly visit their assigned public school, seek out principals, and discuss issues facing their liaison school. Board members should then be asked to report to the whole board about their visitations. At the same time, Dr. Kelly could establish a common administrative council, consisting of public and non-public principals to meet regularly, develop potential common professional development opportunities, and discuss issues of common concern. The Superintendent could also schedule public work sessions to clarify what issues are exclusive to private and public schools and what issues are common to both.

(5) This strategy is designed to break down barriers to communication about how each school community operates, so that each parent community could better understand one another.

Case 23

Dr. Lynn Garrett is the Assistant Superintendent for Business of a rural school district. Dr. Garrett was approached by the local chamber of commerce. They wanted to contribute funds to the school district for specific projects of interest to their members. Dr. Garrett asked that the president of the chamber of commerce meet with the Superintendent and her to discuss how to establish this giving program. The Superintendent suggested that the district establish an educational foundation to support public education with foundation board members selected from the district administrators and community business members. As Assistant Superintendent for Business, Dr. Garrett was not happy with this configuration and sought the advice of the district's legal counsel who indicated that no current district employee could serve as a member of the foundation. Dr. Garrett advised the Superintendent of this legal opinion and he did not concur. The Superintendent called Dr. Garrett into his office with a directive to launch the foundation. Moreover, he appointed Dr. Garrett as the temporary chairperson. Reluctantly, Dr. Garrett adhered to the Superintendent's directive to serve as temporary chair until the foundation met to elect a permanent chair.

Directions:

Read the case carefully, and respond using scenario 2: (1) What did the administrator do well? (2) What did the administrator do poorly? (3) What are three actions the administrator might take to resolve the problem? and (4) Explain why each action is likely to be effective.

Response:

(1) The Assistant Superintendent for Business consulted with the Superintendent when approached by the local chamber of commerce about providing financial support to the schools. Additionally, Dr. Garrett consulted with the district's counsel for a legal opinion regarding the foundation and its relationship with the school district.

(2) The Assistant Superintendent for Business should have proactively sought legal counsel to summarize regulations and present the foundation option along with others to the Superintendent. This would have avoided the Superintendent's position from being stated to a Chamber of Commerce official as a knowledgeable, well-informed opinion.

(3) Three actions the Assistant Superintendent for Business might take to resolve this issue:

- Dr. Garrett should inform the Superintendent that as temporary chair she would seek direction from legal counsel to make sure the foundation has been established within legal guidelines. She would issue a written report to foundation members, the Superintendent, and the Board of Education if current procedures were appropriate.
- Dr. Garrett, upon advice from counsel, should set up a meeting with the Superintendent, president of the chamber of commerce, district's legal counsel, and establish legal parameters for operating the foundation until a permanent chair was selected.
- Dr. Garrett should set up a meeting of the foundation as soon as possible to elect a permanent chair for the foundation.

(4)   It is important that all participants involved with the community foundation act ethically and responsibly within the guidelines of the law so that the foundation is appropriately established.

<u>Case 24</u>

The owner of a local car repair shop with an idea approached Dr. Michael Rosen, Assistant Superintendent of a suburban community near a large city, while he was servicing his car. An article had appeared in the local newspaper regarding the district's falling graduation rate; five years ago, the graduation rate from high school was 86% while this past year the graduation rate was 78%. The repair shop owner said that he and several of his fellow business owners would be willing to create student internships in their businesses to promote careers in the community. It was their belief that having this internship would encourage more students to remain in school and complete their graduation requirements. Dr. Rosen indicated that he would bring the matter to the attention of the Superintendent and Board of Education. If they approved, he would set up an exploratory meeting with business owners, high school administrators and himself to discuss developing an internship program.

<u>Directions:</u>

Read the case carefully, and respond using scenario 3: (1) identify two key issues in the case, (2) give one strategy you might employ to resolve each issue identified, and (3) explain how that strategy might be effective in resolving the issues.

<u>Response:</u>

(1) Two key issues for Dr. Rosen in this case are:
- Falling graduation rates from 86% to 78% have raised concern in the community.
- Establishing an exploratory committee to develop an internship program without addressing the major issue of falling graduation rates is unsound.

(2) A strategy that Dr. Rosen might employ to address each issue:
- Upon consultation with the Superintendent, Dr. Rosen should establish a district committee to investigate the falling graduation rate. This committee should include high school administrative staff, high school teachers, district administrators, parents, community members, and the Board of Education. The committee should examine the decline in graduation rates, look at longitudinal achievement scores, and establish pathways for improvement.
- Dr. Rosen should also establish a career development committee with the local business leaders and high school administrators to

investigate how student internships might be effectively implemented.

(3) This strategy might be effective in addressing these issues because while examining the decline in graduation rates, the district can begin an alternative education program that might help a component of the high school population become successful.

Chapter 5

Standard 5: *to act with integrity, fairness, and in an ethical manner*

Chapter 5

Standard 5: *to act with integrity, fairness, and in an ethical manner*

School based case studies:

Case 25

Ms. Susan Brown is the newly assigned middle school principal that received a letter from the parents of a youngster having academic difficulties. The letter stated that they could no longer afford paying their child's teacher for after school tutoring and requested assistance from the principal. Ms. Brown investigated the assertion in the letter by discussing the issue of after school tutoring with other administrators and various teachers at the middle school. She discovered that teachers regularly tutored their own students (at \$100/hour). This has become a common practice especially among math and science teachers for the past 5+ years. Ms. Brown asked herself, "Is that ethical?"

Directions:

Read the case carefully, and respond using scenario 1: (1) establish one strength of the administrator, (2) give one strategy for building on this strength, (3) indicate one weakness of the administrator, (4) give a strategy for addressing that weakness, and (5) knowing this information, why might these strategies be effective in resolving the case.

Response:

(1) A strength of Ms. Brown is that she investigated the issue before making a decision. She asked other administrators and several teachers about after school tutoring of their own students.

(2) A strategy that the principal might employ regarding this information would be discussing after school tutoring with her fellow principals and the Superintendent to ascertain if there was a district policy about teachers tutoring their own students. If such a policy existed, the principal has a case for enforcing a standing policy. If no such policy exists, the principal should consult with the Superintendent about the unethical nature of this circumstance before taking action.

(3) A weakness of Ms. Brown is that she did not know that after school tutoring by teachers with their own students involving rather hefty fees was a common practice for at least five years in her building. As a new

administrator, it is not a given that Ms. Brown would have developed a working knowledge of all practices in the district. This incident proved to expand her awareness of district practices and formulate some professional opinions.

(4) A strategy the principal might employ to address this weakness is meeting with the other building administrators to find out other unethical practices taking place within the building. The principal should make known to the staff via a faculty meeting that tutoring their own students is unethical. Hopefully there is a Board of Education resolution and/or Superintendent directive supporting her contention. In addition, the principal should issue a memorandum to staff indicating that teachers notify her about any compensation program-taking place before or after school involving students they teach.

(5) In providing information about this circumstance to staff, the principal can reinforce that teachers tutoring their own children after school for remuneration is unacceptable and unethical.

Case 26

Dr. Jeffrey Jones is the principal of a mid-sized suburban high school with a population of 1250 students. One day at dismissal, a female student, Miranda, reported an incident to Dr. Jones. Miranda told Dr. Jones that she had an argument with her English teacher, Mrs. Smith, at dismissal. She said that she cursed Mrs. Smith who then slapped her in the face. Another female student who was with Miranda at dismissal corroborated her story. Both girls stated that another teacher, Ms. Jones, was walking down the corridor at dismissal and had witnessed the incident. Dr. Jones contacted Ms. Jones, the teacher who allegedly witnessed the incident, and asked her if she saw anything unusual at dismissal. Ms. Jones denied seeing anything out of the ordinary. Meanwhile, Dr. Jones obtained written statements from both girls that Ms. Jones was standing in the hallway where the incident took place at dismissal. Dr. Jones directed Ms. Jones to meet him in his office the next morning.

Directions:

Read the case carefully, and respond using scenario 2: (1) what did the administrator do well, (2) what did the administrator do poorly, (3) three actions the administrator might take to resolve the problem, and (4) why each action is likely to be effective.

Response:

(1) Dr. Jones interviewed and obtained written statements from both female students regarding the incident and interviewed Ms. Jones, the teacher who was the alleged witness to the incident.

(2) Dr. Jones should have taken a written statement from both teachers involved in the incident, Mrs. Smith, the teacher who allegedly slapped the student as well as from Ms. Jones, the teacher who allegedly witnessed the incident. Additionally, the principal should have contacted the parents of both female students immediately after the incident was reported to him indicating that he was investigating an incident that allegedly took place during dismissal the other day and would get back to them when his investigation was complete.

(3) Three actions to resolve the problem:
- Meet with Miranda and her parents indicating how her behavior was inappropriate and apply an appropriate behavioral consequence as per the school's discipline code. Dr. Jones can reassure the student and her parents that an appropriate

consequence would be applied to all teachers involved if they acted inappropriately.

- Interview Ms. Jones and Mrs. Smith separately and obtain a written statement as to the extent of their involvement in the incident.
- Bring the incident to the attention of the Superintendent for direction and input from the district's legal counsel.
- Set a second meeting with Mrs. Smith and Ms. Jones separately along with their union representative detailing the facts the principal determined and consequences regarding the incident.

(4) Because the principal diligently pursued the veracity of the incident, obtained substantiation and provided consequences to all guilty parties, the incident could be considered equitably resolved.

<u>Case 27</u>
Dr. Ralph King was the principal of a high school located in a suburb of a major city. One day Dr. King arrived at school earlier than usual and, as he walked through the main office, he saw one of the school social workers with two parents in the deans' office looking at a student's files. Later, when he questioned the social worker about the meeting with the parents in the dean's office, the social worker explained that she was giving the parents therapy outside of school (at $100/hour) and that their youngster had recently gotten into trouble in school. She was helping the parents understand the details of the incident. When Dr. King return to his office, he checked with the Superintendent who confirmed that board policy prohibited professionals from working, tutoring and/or counseling their students and/or their families in the school in which they were employed. Dr. King found out that the parents had battled with the dean over their son's guilt and the consequences imposed. The parents were still not satisfied with the outcome.

<u>Directions:</u>
Read the case carefully, and respond using scenario 3: (1) identify two key issues in the case, (2) give one strategy you might employ to resolve each issue identified, and (3) explain how that strategy might be effective in resolving the issues.

<u>Response:</u>
(1) Two key issues in this case are:
- The school social worker was providing out of school therapy for a fee to parents of a student in the school, which she worked.
- The school social worker was going through the dean's office confidential files and potentially sharing confidential information with the parents of a student who was involved in a disciplinary matter.

(2) A strategy that might resolve each issue is to meet with the school social worker and discuss the unethical nature of her relationship with parents in the school setting. Such a discussion would include informing the social worker that charging a fee for counseling parents of students she worked with during the school day was prohibited by board policy. Additionally, Dr. King needed to inform the social worker that going through disciplinary files in the dean's office was a breach of confidentiality. Parents have a right to see their children's files under the Freedom of Information Law. Files must be appropriately requested

before being released to the parents. Dr. King should then issue a memorandum to all staff reinforcing the district's policy regarding tutoring or counseling students and/or their parents whom they work with during the school year.

(3) This strategy would be effective because it places the school social worker on notice that unethical and unprofessional conduct could result in additional consequences and/or termination.

Case 28

Dr. Alfred Farmer was selected to fill the vacancy for Superintendent by the Board of Education five years ago. He is a dynamic, responsive, and caring Superintendent. The Board of Education gives him their full support. Two years ago, Superintendent Farmer recommended Frank Russo for the Assistant Superintendent for Business vacancy in the district. Frank's resume spoke to his outstanding service in two other school districts as Assistant Superintendent and Business Manager. During the selection process, Frank clearly came away as the premier candidate for the position because of his integrity and knowledge of business functions. The Superintendent and Assistant Superintendent became fast friends, respecting each other's abilities and responsibilities. One day, the Superintendent requested that the Assistant Superintendent arrange for a custodial worker to purchase his daily newspaper as well as have his car washed weekly. The Superintendent reasoned that the district should fund these expenditures because he used his car to travel around the district and he needed to keep abreast of the daily news that might affect the district's functioning. The Assistant Superintendent was uncomfortable with ordering this to be done.

Directions:

Read the case carefully, and respond using scenario 1: (1) establish one strength of the Assistant Superintendent, (2) give one strategy for building on this strength, (3) indicate one weakness of the assistant superintendent, (4) give a strategy for addressing that weakness, and (5) knowing this information, why might these strategies be effective in resolving the case.

Response:

(1) The Assistant Superintendent was selected for this position because of his outstanding reputation, perceived integrity, and expertise in business functions having served as an Assistant Superintendent for Business and Business Manager in other school districts.

(2) Since the Assistant Superintendent has a reputation of integrity and expertise, he should approach the Superintendent with his concern, namely that purchasing the daily newspaper and washing the Superintendent's car are expenditures that would not stand up to scrutiny under audit, no matter what the Superintendent says.

(3)   Because of the relationship Superintendent Farmer had with Frank Russo, Frank was eager to fulfill his responsibilities. However, by the Superintendent asking an employee to purchase his daily newspaper and have his car washed, the Superintendent was playing on their friendship to pursue his personal agenda. The Assistant Superintendent wanted to maintain a positive relationship with the Superintendent; after all, the Superintendent was instrumental in his selection. However, Frank was put in an unethical position and he needs to be honest and forthright with the Superintendent.

(4)   A strategy that Frank Russo could employ might be to address the Superintendent on a personal level, informing him that requesting an employee to purchase his daily newspaper and wash his car are outside the roles and responsibilities of custodial workers and surely appears to look unethical. Frank should inform the Superintendent that an auditor would take exception with the employee's function and the district's expenditure for a daily newspaper and weekly car washes.

(5)   This strategy might resolve this issue because using a friendship established between the Superintendent and the Assistant Superintendent for Business might lessen the tension created by the Superintendent's inappropriate demands for use of a district employee and inappropriate use of public funds.

Case 29

The high school wrestling coach of an outstanding wrestling program had a problem. Although wrestlers in his program won many awards and graduated as outstanding student athletes, the Athletic Director informed the coach that the Superintendent wanted to move the wrestling room and weight training room out of their current locations into other spaces because the Superintendent wanted to implement a new dance program. The wrestling program had used the current rooms for the past 12 years. The Athletic Director and coach looked at the replacement rooms in the basement of the building. The wrestling coach concluded that the space to be provided was clearly inferior. The coach truly believed that the wrestling program would suffer from this displacement. The Athletic Director refused to intercede on the coach's behalf with the Superintendent. The Athletic Director indicated that the alternative space would be adequate and he further indicated that the program would receive new wrestling mats and additional weight training equipment as a result. The wrestling coach still felt the children were being shortchanged and deprived of an appropriate training space so he reached out to the Wrestling Moms and Dads Club and shared the problem with them. The Athletic Director also spoke with representatives of the Wrestling Moms and Dads Club, indicating that the move would not be that bad. However, representatives of the Wrestling Moms and Dads Club did not believe the Athletic Director and spoke out at the next public Board of Education meeting about how detrimental moving the wrestling program would be. The Board of Education members were sympathetic to the parents and ordered the Superintendent to provide additional financial resources and an adequate space for the wrestling program that would satisfy the needs of both programs. The Superintendent was furious with the wrestling coach.

Directions:

Read the case carefully, and respond using scenario 2: (1) what did the administrator (Athletic Director) do well, (2) what did the administrator do poorly, (3) three actions the administrator might take to resolve the problem, and (4) why each action is likely to be effective.

Response:

(1) The Athletic Director, as part of the district administrative team, supported the Superintendent's decision to move the wrestling program in order to implement a new dance program. Although he initially met with the wrestling coach and looked at alternate spaces for the program with the

coach, he indicated that the initial alternate space identified by the Superintendent would be adequate.

(2) The Athletic Director lacked effective communication skills. Because he did not advocate for the wrestling program, he did not maintain the confidence of his wrestling coach and/or the Wrestling Moms and Dads Club. Additionally, he could have taken the initiative and involved the high school principal in identifying alternate spaces that were satisfactory for the wrestling program. Moreover, he should have discussed the issue with the Superintendent and provided him with alternatives prior to the public Board of Education meeting.

(3) Three actions the Athletic Director might have take to resolve the issue:
- Set up a meeting with the wrestling coach to clearly communicate his support for the wrestling program and work collaboratively with the coach to identify alternate spaces to house the wrestling program.
- Meet with the Wrestling Moms and Dads Club to assure them that he would support an appropriate space that was satisfactory to conduct a successful wrestling program.
- Set up a meeting with the Superintendent, Wrestling Moms and Dads Club, and wrestling coach to work out an amicable solution of the issue prior to the Board of Education meeting.

(4) These actions would be effective because they would have avoided the outcry by the Wrestling Moms and Dads Club at a public Board of Education meeting, causing dissention among the Board of Education members and anger by the Superintendent that his/her directive was not followed.

Case 30

Mr. Pete Cameron is the Athletic Director of an affluent school district having an outstanding athletic program with many competitive teams. The Superintendent and Assistant Superintendent have supported the athletic program in past years. However, the athletic teams' facilities are less than adequate. The boys' and girls' team locker rooms have many non-functioning showers, broken lockers, cracked tile, and poor lighting. One day during the fall football season, the head football coach approached the Athletic Director with a dilemma. The Board of Education president's son was a player on the varsity football team but did not qualify as a starter. Knowing the problems with the facilities, the head coach proposed to the Athletic Director that he make the youngster a starter so that dad would be aware of the poor conditions on and off the field and thereby become more of an advocate for repair and upgrade of the athletic facilities.

Directions:

Read the case carefully, and respond as the Athletic Director using scenario 3: (1) identify two key issues in the case, (2) give one strategy you might employ to resolve each issue identified, and (3) explain how that strategy might be effective in resolving the issues.

Response:

(1) Two key issues in this case are:

- Although the district supported a comprehensive athletic program, the athletic facilities are inadequate and in a state of disrepair.
- The head football coach approached the Athletic Director to present an unethical solution to an existing problem.

(2) The Athletic Director should request a meeting with the Superintendent and Board of Education members to discuss disrepair of the athletic facilities. With the support of the Superintendent, the Athletic Director could work with a Board of Education member to outline necessary repairs and appropriate timeframes for their completion. More importantly, the Athletic Director should meet with all coaches outlining appropriate ethical practice in all coaching situations.

(3) By sharing expectations with coaches, the Athletic Director is modeling and setting appropriate behavioral expectations at the highest ethical level for all coaches.

Chapter 6

Standard 6: *to understand, respond to, and influence the larger political, social, economic, legal and cultural context*

Chapter 6

Standard 6: *to understand, respond to, and influence the larger political, social, economic, legal and cultural context.*

School based case studies:

Case 31
The principal of a middle school is chairing an interview committee charged with finding the best candidate for a probationary teaching position in mathematics. The committee has interviewed six candidates and found that all would be suitable. However, one candidate has emerged far above the rest. She clearly has more experience, enthusiasm, warmth, and intelligence than other candidates do. Additionally, her writing sample and demonstration lesson were superior. The problem is that she has intolerably strong body odor, so strong that the students in the class where she did her demonstration lesson leaned away from her as she taught. Because she did her demonstration lesson and completed her writing sample on the same day that she was interviewed, the principal was not certain if her body odor was temporary, recurrent, or a permanent condition. The committee looked to the principal for direction because it was concerned about discrimination against this candidate for a condition that she may not be able to control. The committee wanted to recommend her to the Superintendent for hiring since she was the very best candidate around.

Directions:
Read the case carefully, and respond using scenario 1: (1) establish one strength of the administrator, (2) give one strategy for building on this strength, (3) indicate one weakness of the administrator, (4) give a strategy for addressing that weakness, and (5) knowing this information, why might these strategies be effective in resolving the case.

Response:
(1) One strength of this principal is the inclusive manner in which he involved a committee in hiring the replacement mathematics teacher. Additionally, the hiring committee looked towards the principal for leadership regarding the body odor issue since they felt comfortable with his leadership style.

(2) A strategy the principal might employ to build on this strength is to call a committee meeting to enlist the support of the committee and have all candidates revisit the school to meet other mathematics teachers. This would provide an opportunity to ascertain if the candidate's body odor was a recurring issue.

(3) The hiring process might be more effective if the principal pre-screened the six candidates before the committee interviewed them. A preliminary screening might have brought the body odor issue to the principal's attention earlier in the process so that the committee would be able to make a more informed decision about that particular candidate.

(4) A strategy for addressing that weakness would include the principal setting up parameters for interviewing candidates prior to the first committee meeting so that a pre-screening would be part of the process.

(5) It would be important to any screening process that the rules and procedures be established before the process begins. With such rules in place, there would be greater transparency in the hiring process.

Case 32

You are the assistant principal in a large high school. A parent charges into your office first thing Monday morning waving papers in her hand and demanding action. After the parent's initial hysteria, you discover that her daughter had been texting over the weekend, and her friends wrote disgusting things about her (mostly of a sexual nature) and made a threat to "expose" her in the locker room during gym class sometime that week. The mother deleted the prompts and responses from her daughter's computer but had the hardcopies, which she printed for you. The mother claims to know the identity of the three or four girls who have been cyber-bullying her daughter and gives you their names. You explained that you would investigate the matter. Later that day, you interviewed the victim as well as the alleged three or four students who were the perpetrators. These girls' vehemently and sincerely (it seemed to you) denied their involvement. You also spoke with the girls' parents. The alleged victim's mother returned first thing Wednesday morning and said: "Thanks a lot, now her daughter doesn't have any friends and hates school." What will you do?

Directions:

Read the case carefully, and respond using scenario 2: (1) what did the administrator do well, (2) what did the administrator do poorly, (3) three actions the administrator might take to resolve the problem, and (4) why each action is likely to be effective.

Response:

(1) The assistant principal interviewed the victim and the alleged perpetrators to get a better handle on the cyber-bullying incident. In addition, the assistant principal spoke with the parents of the girls involved.

(2) The assistant principal should have shared the incident with the principal and Superintendent to determine if the police should be involved. Cyber-crime is a police matter. The police would indicate whether to continue the investigation with or without them as participants. The assistant principal could re-interview the alleged perpetrators individually to ascertain where they were when the alleged incident took place and who was with them at that time. Corroboration could be obtained by interviewing friends and family.

(3) Three actions the assistant principal might take to resolve the problem:

- The assistant principal can meet with each of the girls involved in the incident and inform them that cyber-bullying is a crime and has potential consequences if convicted.
- The assistant principal could threaten a variety of consequences from in-school detention or suspension to out of school suspension depending on the district's discipline code if any repeated event takes place.
- The assistant principal could also set up a program about cyber-bulling for all parents and children at the high school.

(4)   Each action when grouped together likely will be an effective deterrent to students' cyber-bullying by pointing out facts and fiction about cyber-bullying, consequences of cyber-bullying and what parents should know about cyber-bullying.

Case 33

You are the assistant principal in charge of discipline for a large high school in a midsized city. One afternoon about 4:30 p.m., a school security officer brought you a boy and a girl whom he caught "making out" under the bleachers. After he told you why he brought these students to you, he pulled you aside and privately told you that they were having oral sex. The school security officer indicated that he watched them for some time and saw that they performed oral sex on one another and that they had kept most of their clothes on. The school security officer went on to joke about how he wished he were a teenager today because sex seemed to be so prevalent and easy to get.

Directions:

Read the case carefully, and respond using scenario 3: (1) identify two key issues in the case, (2) give one strategy you might employ to resolve each issue identified, and (3) explain how that strategy might be effective in resolving the issues.

Response

(1) Two key issues in this case:

- Two minors were allegedly engaging in a sex act on school grounds.
- The school security officer observed the sex taking place for an extended period before taking action.

(2) A strategy you might employ to resolve these issues is to involve parents and the police department with regard to the sex act. After thoroughly investigating the incident and obtaining written statements from both students and the school security officer, the assistant principal should involve the principal and Superintendent for further direction. At that point, the police should be involved in this case. The parents of the students involved in the incident must also be informed and a disciplinary hearing set for both students. Additionally, a disciplinary hearing must be set for the school security officer who inappropriately handled the incident by his delayed intervention, chose to observe the sex act before apprehending the students, and inappropriately commented about what took place to the assistant principal.

(3) The students and their parents have to understand that committing a sex act although consensual, is unacceptable, unlawful, and has consequences. By applying fair and equal consequences to both students,

the school population will understand that inappropriate behavior is unacceptable and will not be sanctioned in school. Likewise, by disciplining the school security officer, it becomes clear that inappropriate behavior is not tolerated.

District based case studies:

Case 34

Superintendent Dr. Bruce Redden was known for his progressive attitude towards bringing new initiatives to the school district. At a recent American Association of School Administrators conference, the Superintendent participated in a workshop given by Dr. Dice who developed a program focused on institutional culture shift. Dr. Redden was so impressed that he brought back the idea to district administrators to share at an administrative council meeting. The Superintendent indicated that he was implementing the program immediately. Dr. Redden wanted to change the culture of the school district by making the district a more vibrant and exciting place to work and learn. He called Dr. Dice and set up a schedule for training all employees to take place over the next twelve months.

Directions:

Read the case carefully, and respond using scenario 1: (1) establish one strength of the administrator, (2) give one strategy for building on this strength, (3) indicate one weakness of the administrator, (4) give a strategy for addressing that weakness, and (5) knowing this information, why might these strategies be effective in resolving the case.

Response:

(1) A strength of Dr. Redden is that he was a progressive Superintendent who believed that status quo for the district was unacceptable and decided that a shift in the organization's culture was necessary.

(2) To build on his desire to change the organization's culture, Dr. Redden should have established a committee of administrators to investigate Dr. Dice's change process as well as other programs that would give similar results. The committee could enlist others in the educational community to be part of the planning process, if the idea for institutional change was warranted.

(3) Dr. Redden's weakness is foregoing participation by constituencies within the district to initiate the change process. He neither consulted with the district administrative team to determine their willingness to become change agents nor asked their opinion about the participation of teachers and other staff to be included in the training program. Additionally, Dr. Redden did not check with the Assistant Superintendent for Business to

see if appropriate funds were available for this program, met comptroller's regulations' compliance, and Board of Education policy compliance.

(4) It is never too late to begin at the beginning, by establishing a committee to investigate the change process and possible organizations that provide such services as Dr. Dice offered. If the concept for change was adopted, the committee could outreach to other district employees, parents, and Board of Education members to become participants in the planning process. At the same time, the Superintendent could work with the Assistant Superintendent for Business to secure funding for this effort.

(5) These strategies might be effective in resolving the issue because change is difficult. Research tells us that the more constituents involved in the process, the greater the chance a cultural shift will be lasting over time.

Case 35

Superintendent Stuart Blank is a progressive, caring and sensitive school district leader. He has a terrific relationship with community members and sits on the Boards of a variety of community organizations including the local Rotary Club. One of the Rotary members approached Dr. Blank and suggested that the business community could raise significant amounts of money to support the arts in the district's K–12 educational program. Superintendent Blank thought that was a terrific idea and with the help of the district's legal counsel established a foundation to support business community initiatives in district schools. The Board of Education adopted a resolution to create the foundation. At the first Board of Directors meeting, the Superintendent suggested that the foundation establish an annual dinner dance and silent auction to begin the fund raising effort. This idea was adopted by the Board of Directors. The Superintendent sent a memorandum to all district administrative staff ordering them to participate in the foundation dinner dance. At the next administrators' meeting, the Superintendent distributed responsibilities to administrators to ensure that the dinner dance was a success. One administrator, Mr. Golden, a building principal with four years of experience in the district, returned his invitation and responsibility directive with a response that he was unavailable to participate in this program. The Superintendent was furious since he assigned Mr. Golden to obtain items for the silent auction. Dr. Blank sent Mr. Golden a letter indicating that his non-participation might adversely affect his end of year rating. After all, reasoned the Superintendent, "we're all part of a team to serve the children of the community." The Superintendent went on that he expected the principal to participate and provide leadership to help make the event successful.

Directions:

Read the case carefully, and respond using scenario 2: (1) what did the administrator do well, (2) what did the administrator do poorly, (3) three actions the administrator might take to resolve the problem, and (4) why each action is likely to be effective.

Response:

(1) Dr. Blank was involved with a variety of community-based organizations, including the local Rotary Club. The Superintendent took on the initiative to create a community-based foundation to support arts programs in the schools.

(2) Dr. Blank was one-tracked on the issue of supporting a successful dinner dance and silent auction. He mandated is administrative staff to participate in a foundation without checking the legality of district employees participating in a non-district run event.

(3) To resolve this problem, Dr. Blank might:
- Call upon the district's counsel to offer an opinion as to whether he could mandate participation of the district's administrative staff in a community held event. With advice from legal counsel, meet with Mr. Golden to resolve their differences.
- Meet with the district's administrators to explain the importance of the foundation to the district's schools, and the potential windfall of support for arts programming the foundation might generate for their respective schools. He could then ask for volunteers.

- Sponsor a meet and greet with the administrators and members of the foundation Board of Directors to generate support for the foundation and foundation-initiated events.

(4) Each of these suggestions is likely to create a positive relationship between the school district's administrative team, the foundation, and the Superintendent.

Case 36

Mrs. Sylvia Barber was selected as Superintendent of an affluent school district five years ago. Dr. Barber was an exceptional dresser who wore expensive suits to work daily. Dr. Barber has the respect and support of the Board of Education, parents and community. Moreover, she has diligently served the school community and participated in many events before, during, and after school. Likewise, achievement levels have significantly improved in all schools under her leadership. One week, while touring the high school, she remarked to her building principal that the attire of the teaching staff was sloppy. Many of the teachers, in her opinion, were unkempt and dressed inappropriately. She ordered her principal to prepare a memorandum to teaching staff directing that professionals dress in alignment with a recent Board of Education policy regarding student attire. The Board of Education policy stated that students' attire must be appropriate and not interfere with instruction. If indeed a student's attire interfered with instruction, as deemed by the building principal, then inappropriate attire could be considered a disciplinary infraction and dealt with accordingly. The Superintendent further indicated to her principal that teachers should be treated as professionals and professionals dress appropriately in the workplace.

Directions:

Read the case carefully, and respond using scenario 3: (1) identify two key issues in the case, (2) give one strategy you might employ to resolve each issue identified, and (3) explain how that strategy might be effective in resolving the issues.

Response:

(1) Two key issues in this case are:
- The Superintendent, Dr. Barber, was well respected by the parents, community, and Board of Education. She always dressed the role of Superintendent, wearing appropriate attire to work every day. Teachers were coming to work inappropriately dressed in the opinion of the Superintendent.
- The Board of Education recently ratified a policy regarding student attire, which prohibited children from coming to school in any attire that would interfere with instruction. The Superintendent wanted this policy applied to the teaching staff.

(2) One strategy that Dr. Barber might employ is to meet with union leadership to share her concerns about teacher attire. This could then be

relayed to the teaching staff. At the same time, the Superintendent could meet with her principals to suggest that staff be appropriately dressed. Dr. Barber might also confer with the district's legal counsel to get appropriate case law information about requiring employees to wear appropriate attire in the workplace.

(3) Issuing a memorandum regarding appropriate attire in the workplace would be ineffective and inappropriate without input regarding its legality and its effect in each school building. By having the administrative staff on board and teacher union representatives in agreement, the Superintendent might avoid issuing a directive that might have spurious results.

Chapter 7

Multiple-Choice Questions

Chapter 7

In-Basket, Multiple Choice Questions

In this chapter, we are asking you to pretend that you are the educational leader in each situation. We would like you to read and react to each "in-basket" item. The items we have included come from our real life experience as administrators. Remember that line administrators, whether district or building based, have to make quick decisions based upon their knowledge, background, expertise and experience. In testing situations, read the question quickly but thoroughly, analyze the possible correct solutions to the situation, and select the response giving the answer, which most likely will resolve the situation or problem. Your first choice is probably the correct response! After each question, we provide the best choice and an explanation for that choice.

Good luck!

Preparing for Educational Leadership

School-based Multiple Choice Questions

Standard 1: _to develop, articulate, implement, and steward a vision of learning_

1. You are the principal of an elementary school where fourth grade English Language Arts (ELA) scores have declined for the past three years. The number of students exhibiting proficiency (level 3 or 4) has dropped from 89% to 85% to 81%. The Superintendent has asked you for an <u>immediate</u> action plan to improve the ELA scores. What is your next step?

A. Order test prep materials and mandate 30 minutes of practice every day.

B. Meet with the fourth grade teachers to discuss why the scores are declining.

C. Disaggregate the data and look for patterns, consult with available staff, write a plan and submit it to the Superintendent.

D. Request the Superintendent give you time to convene a committee, with you as a member, that includes teachers across the grade levels and charge the committee to investigate declining scores at each grade level, take input from a variety of sources, and then develop an action plan.

Answer: C

Explanation:
Since the Superintendent has asked you for a plan in a short period, the best answer is C. If you were given ample time to convene a committee, D would be the best answer.

2. You are a high school principal. A parent complains that her child's teacher is frequently absent. She wants to know what you are going to do about it to assure continuity of instruction. It is a Regents class and she is concerned that her child will be unprepared for the exam. What should you do next?

A. Tell the parent that the teacher has a medical condition that prevents her from coming to work every day.

B. Let her know that you are aware of the problem and that you are working with the teacher to improve her attendance.

C. Inform the parent that people have a right to be sick.

D. Transfer the child to the class of a teacher with better attendance.

Answer: B

Explanation:
Absence is a difficult problem to deal with because teachers contractually do not have to submit a doctor's note until they have been absent a specified number of consecutive days. Let the parent know that you are working with the teacher to improve her attendance. Assure the parent that you will take appropriate steps so that her child will be properly prepared for the Regents exam.

3. A female student alleges that her remedial reading teacher stated that she is behaving like an animal. When you, the principal, meet with the reading teacher to discuss the student's allegation, the reading teacher states that there was an animal character in the reading selection and the student misunderstood her statement. What action do you take?

A. Interview all the students in the reading group and then decide whether the allegation is true.

B. Tell the student that she misunderstood what the teacher said.

C. Meet with the union representative to discuss the allegation.

D. Meet with the teacher and the student to discuss the matter.

Answer: A

Explanation:
When a student alleges that a teacher spoke inappropriately about her, an administrator should investigate the matter properly and promptly. If the teacher's statement differs from statements taken from students individually, the principal must make a determination. If the principal feels that students' versions reflect what really transpired, the principal must take disciplinary action against the teacher.

Standard 2: *to promote the success of all students, promote a positive school culture, provide an effective instructional program, apply best practice to student learning, and design comprehensive professional growth plans for staff*

1. You are the principal. A student comes home from school and tells his parent that his teacher grabbed his arm and twisted it. His father asks why this happened and the boy says that he was fooling around and not paying attention. The father comes up to see you. He demands that the teacher be fired. How would you respond?

A. Tell the father that since his son was misbehaving, it was okay for the teacher to grab his son's arm to get his attention.

B. Schedule a conference with the teacher, the father and you.

C. Write down the father's allegations and tell him that you will get back to him after you investigate the incident.

D. Ask the teacher why she did it and then have her apologize to the student.

Answer: C

Explanation:
When a student informs a parent about an incident that occurred in school, many parents assume that everything the child stated is accurate. An administrator must collect evidence from the parties and witnesses involved, review the information and make an informed judgment. The principal should assure the parent that the matter would be investigated immediately and the parent contacted as soon as all of the facts have been gathered. The principal should get statements from the alleged victim, the teacher, and anyone else who witnessed the alleged incident. Give the parent a date when you would get back to him so that he will not consider contacting the Superintendent while you are investigating the incident.

2. A parent contacts her child's principal to protest the English grade her daughter received on her report card. The parent demands a conference with the principal and the classroom teacher. The parent informs the principal that she will be bringing her sister who is an English teacher in a neighboring high school to the meeting. How should the principal first react?

A. Inform the parent that the principal will meet with her but not with her sister.

B. Ask the parent if she has discussed her daughter's grade with the English teacher.

C. Set up the conference with the parent, her sister, the teacher, and the principal.

D. The principal should meet with the teacher, discuss the grade, and then meet with the parent and her sister without the teacher present.

Answer: B

Explanation:
All initial conversations should be directly with the teacher. Inform the parent that she may come back to you if she is not satisfied with the outcome of the discussion with the teacher. Parents may bring anyone they desire to advocate on their behalf or to observe a meeting.

3. The Superintendent instructs you, the principal, to cut 10% from the extracurricular club budget for next year immediately. You have thirty-five clubs with forty-eight advisors and co-advisors. How do you decide which clubs and/or advisors to cut?

A. Analyze the attendance for each club and take into account politically sensitive clubs when deciding which clubs to cut or which clubs should not have a co-advisor.

B. Cut back on clubs with co-advisors.

C. Cut out clubs with the lowest average attendance.

D. Discuss the merit of each club with your school leadership team.

Answer: A

Explanation:
Clubs with lowest attendance should be discontinued or co-advisors cut unless the club is politically sensitive. Since the Superintendent requested an immediate response, discussion in reductions of extra-curricular clubs by the leadership team is not possible. It is important to take into consideration terms of the teachers' collective bargaining agreement with regard to clubs with advisors and co-advisors.

4. A parent contacts you to contest her daughter's Spanish grade. The parent contends that the teacher did not like her daughter and punished her by giving her a grade lower than the one she deserved. As principal, what is your first step?

A. Ask the parent what evidence she has that indicates her daughter was not graded fairly.

B. Inform the parent that she has to discuss the grade with her child's teacher first before you get involved.

C. Contact the teacher to discuss her grading rubric.

D. Change the grade if you feel that the teacher has not graded the child appropriately.

Answer: B

Explanation:
The parent should discuss the grade with the teacher first. If the parent still feels that her child was graded unfairly, an administrator should meet with the teacher and ask her to demonstrate with her rubric how the child's grade was determined. The principal should weigh the evidence and decide if the grade was given fairly. Principals have a legal write to change grades with cause.

5. You are the principal of a large high school. The Superintendent informs you that, due to budgetary constraints, you will have to reduce your teaching staff by six positions for next year. What is your first step?

A) Meet with your assistant principals and tell them that you had to cut six teaching positions.

B) Work with staff collaboratively to look for places to cut positions while providing options to reduce the budget in non-teaching areas.

C) Meet with the Superintendent and tell him that you are not cutting the budget because it is not in the best interest of the children.

D) Establish a committee to discuss the impending budget cut and have the committee study how to reduce the budget.

Answer: B

Explanation:
Decision-making that involves participation has the most value to an organization because constituency participation tends to make the decision lasting and "stick" in that organization.

Standard 3: *to ensure management of the organization, operations, and resources for a safe, efficient, and effective learning environment*

1. You are the principal of an elementary school and a parent schedules an appointment to meet with you. She states that her child's third grade teacher does not check homework at all. The parent feels that it is the teacher's responsibility to review homework in order to know how each child is performing in her class. How do you respond?

A. Tell the parent that each teacher sets her own policy for checking homework.

B. Inform the parent that you will meet with the teacher and then call her.

C. Ask the parent to speak to the teacher first and then, if not satisfied, to come back and see you.

D. Notify the parent that you will discuss homework policy at the next faculty meeting.

Answer: C

Explanation:
There is a proper chain of command. Most parental concerns about a teacher's practice should be handled by the teacher first. The principal should let the parent know that if she is not satisfied with the teacher's explanation that she should then make an appointment with you. The principal should inform the teacher to expect a call and/or visit from the parent.

2. A female student told her Guidance Counselor that a male student inappropriately touched her during passing. She stated that this boy has done this to many girls; the other girls never reported it. The Guidance Counselor brought this matter to the principal's attention. If you were the principal, what would your first step be?

A. Have the Guidance Counselor investigate the allegation and report to you.

B. Summon the male student to your office and ask him if he did it.

C. Interview the female and male students separately, take copious notes and ask for the names of witnesses.

D. Call the girl's mother to let her know what happened.

Answer: C

Explanation:
Inappropriate touching is a form of sexual harassment and is a very serious matter. An administrator should investigate this matter immediately by taking statements from the two students involved in the alleged incident as well as any possible witnesses. If witnesses confirm the boy's action, he should be dealt with in an appropriate manner. If it is a "he said – she said" situation with no witnesses, the principal cannot ascertain that the male student committed this action. Additionally, the girl's parents should have been contacted when she reported the incident. Likewise, the boy's parents should be notified about the allegation as well. Even if you have no concrete evidence that the boy touched the girl, it would be a good idea to have a Guidance Counselor speak with him about this issue.

3. A teacher informs the assistant principal that she has been collecting money for a class trip. When she arrived in her classroom, she discovered that the envelope with the $250 trip money was taken from her desk drawer. She wants the assistant principal to pay for the trip with school funds. What does the assistant principal do first?

A. Ask the Parent Organization to pay for the trip.

B. Pay for the trip from school funds.

C. Inform the teacher that she should have brought the money to the office each day to be secured in the school safe.

D. Tell the teacher that although you sympathize with her loss, she has to pay for the trip from personal funds because the school is not responsible for money not secured according to school regulations and left in a teacher's drawer.

Answer: D

Explanation:
Teachers have been informed of the standard school policy about collecting funds; all money collected should be brought to the office daily. Teachers get receipts for the money they bring to the office to put into the school's safe. If a teacher disregards the policy and leaves money in a drawer, locked or unlocked, she would be responsible for replacing any money that was stolen or misplaced.

4. A school bus driver reports that there has been frequent fighting on the bus. One of the students opened the Emergency Door and threw another student's backpack out of the moving bus. What course of action should the principal take?

A. Immediately suspend the child who tossed the book bag for committing a dangerous action.

B. Suspend both children for fighting.

C. Investigate the incident and suspend the instigator.

D. Check each student's file to see if the student committed any other bus infractions this year before deciding on a punishment.

Answer: A

Explanation:
An investigation should determine what happened on the bus. Statements should be taken from the driver and other children who witnessed the incident. A dangerous action such as opening the Emergency Door on a moving school bus should result in an immediate consequence, a suspension from school as well as a bus suspension. If the bus had a video recording system, use the video in your investigatory process.

Preparing for Educational Leadership

5. A teacher informs you, the principal, that another teacher is releasing her students prior to the end of the period. These noisy students are standing in the hall and disturbing the other classes. How would you resolve this situation?

A. Send the teacher a memo reminding her to keep the students in the room until the bell rings.

B. Tell the first teacher not to notify you about another teacher's conduct.

C. Observe the hall at dismissal and meet with the teacher afterward to discuss her early dismissal.

D. Ask students if their teacher is dismissing them before the bell.

Answer: C

Explanation:
An administrator should observe the situation to determine if the teacher is releasing her students before the bell sounds. Let the teacher who reported the incident know that you are investigating her allegations and will get back to her. If the teacher is releasing the students too early, inform her in a friendly manner that students cannot be released from class until the bell rings.

6. During the annual Talent Show, a group of students perform a song with lyrics that offend gay and lesbian students. The students sang different lyrics during rehearsals. What action would you take as principal?

A. Have the students offer a public apology at an assembly.

B. Suspend the students who sang the offensive lyrics.

C. Arrange a meeting with the students' parents as soon as possible.

D. Tell the Talent Show advisor that he should have had better control over the content of the show.

Answer: B

Explanation:
The students should be suspended for committing a purposeful act by changing the lyrics from the lyrics they sang during rehearsal to the lyrics they sang during the show that they knew would offend gay and lesbian students.

7. A female student tells her Guidance Counselor that a nude picture of her was emailed to many students by her ex-boyfriend from his home computer. The girl stated that she had let him take the picture of her when they were dating. The Guidance Counselor apprised the principal of this situation. As principal, what would you do first?

A. Suspend the boy immediately.

B. Notify the police.

C. Call the girl's parents to discuss what happened.

D. Ban the male student from using the school's computer.

Answer: C

Explanation:
The girl's parents should be contacted immediately to let them know what happened. The principal should then contact the boy's parents to make them aware of the allegation. An investigation should take place to ascertain if the allegation is true. If the incident was discussed in school or involved the use of school equipment, the principal has greater latitude in disciplining the student. The police should be involved as well.

8. You are the principal of a high school who arrives at work at 7:00 AM on a cold winter morning only to discover that the boiler that heats half the building is not functioning. The Head Custodian informs you that the problem cannot be corrected until a technician arrives later in the day. What action do you take?

A. Contact the Superintendent immediately and discuss an emergency evacuation plan.

B. Immediately create a schedule that doubles up the number of students in every classroom so that only the heated rooms are used.

C. Go about your regular schedule and instruct the students to keep their coats on.

D. Contact parents so that they can come to school to pick up their children.

Answer: A

Explanation:
Schools have contingency plans that go into effect when a building or part of it cannot be used due to a mechanical failure or natural disaster. The Superintendent will give the principal the authority to put the alternate site plan into effect.

9. A teacher calls the principal's office and states there is a smell of smoke on the second floor. Your secretary immediately informs you of this call. What action do you take?

A. Pull the fire alarm to evacuate the building.

B. Go up to the second floor and investigate the situation.

C. Have the custodian investigate the odor.

D. Evacuate students from the second floor only.

Answer: A

Explanation:
When someone reports a smoky condition, the building should be evacuated immediately. The fire department will decide what occurred and when the building is safe to re-enter.

Standard 4: *to collaborate with families and community members, to respond to diverse community interests and needs, and to mobilize community resources*

1. A father calls the principal's office and indicates that his family has been evicted from their home and placed in a homeless shelter in another school district 10 miles away. The parent wants his child to continue to attend your school. The parent tells the principal that he expects the school district to pay $15 per day for cab fare for his children to continue to attend your school. How do you respond?

A. Inform the parent that children have to attend school in the district in which they currently reside.

B. Notify the parent that the child can still attend the school if the parent can transport the child to school.

C. Tell the parent to contact social services.

D. Inform the parent that transportation will be arranged at the district's expense for his children to continue to attend your school.

Answer: D

Explanation:
Federal law states that the school district must pay for transportation costs when a family that resided in the district becomes homeless and is living in a shelter in another district.

2. A father who was not chosen to be a chaperone (by luck of the draw) on a second grade school trip notifies his child's teacher that he will be at the destination anyway to escort his child. He feels that his daughter will be uncomfortable chaperoned by another parent. The teacher discusses this with you, the principal. What is your first step?

A. Notify the father that it is permissible for him to go to the destination on his own and chaperone his daughter.

B. Permit the father to go on the bus with the class and act as a chaperone for a group.

C. Allow the father to get there independently and then chaperone a group of students.

D. Inform the father that he cannot come near the class on the trip because he was not selected as a chaperone.

Answer: D

Explanation:
A parent who was not chosen as a chaperone cannot interact with his child or other children on a class trip. Notify the parent that if he is not comfortable with his daughter being chaperoned by other parents, he can keep his daughter from participating in the trip. She would be assigned to another class in that grade to assure her continuity of instruction for the day.

Standard 5: *to act with integrity, fairness, and in an ethical manner*

1. The Parent Organization president informs the principal that she has received numerous complaints from parents about a teacher, Mrs. Smith. She states that parents are complaining that the teacher is unprepared and often talks on her cell phone while students are in the room. What is the principal's first action?

A. Thank the Parent Organization president for this information and let her know that you will look into the matter.

B. Speak to Mrs. Smith about these allegations.

C. Inform the Parent Organization president that you cannot discuss a teacher's behavior because such matters are confidential and she does not have a child in that class.

D. Interview students to determine if Mrs. Smith uses her cell phone in class.

Answer: C

Explanation:
You can only speak to the Parent Organization president about a teacher if she has a child in that class. Parents may give permission for someone else to represent them in a conversation about a teacher. Many Parent Organization presidents feel that they have the right to discuss teachers' behaviors because they serve as an elected representative of the parent body. Under the Privacy Act (FERPA), administrators may only speak with parents about situations involving their own children.

2. During recess, a child falls and cuts his leg. The teacher calls the mother to report the accident and tells her that the injury was due to broken pavement that the district did not want to spend $20,000 to repair. The teacher suggests that the parent sue the school district. The teacher left for the day without filing an accident report. A lawsuit is filed two weeks later. What, as principal, should you do first?

A. Give the teacher a disciplinary letter for her file because she suggested to the parent that the parent file a lawsuit.

B. Give the teacher a disciplinary letter for her file because she did not report an accident.

C. Give the teacher a disciplinary letter for her file because she suggested the lawsuit and for failure to report an accident.

D. Try to talk the parent out of suing the school district.

Answer: B

Explanation:
The teacher should receive a disciplinary letter for her file because she was negligent in not reporting an accident. Although she was unprofessional in suggesting a lawsuit to the parent, she did not violate the collective bargaining agreement or district policy.

3. You are a principal who suspends a male student for his involvement in a fight in the cafeteria. You notify the parent by telephone and in writing that the child is suspended from attending school for three days. The parent refuses to accept the suspension and states that she is sending her son to school tomorrow anyway and, in addition, she is calling the Superintendent to complain about your actions. What do you do?

A. Notify the parent that there will be a suspension hearing in your office tomorrow morning at 8:00 A.M.

B. Tell her that the Superintendent does not overturn principal suspensions.

C. Reduce the suspension to one day in an effort to find a common ground with the parent.

D. Recommend anger management counseling for the student.

Answer: A

Explanation:
Parents and students have a right to a suspension hearing. Inform the parent, in writing, that the suspension stands pending a formal hearing. Schedule the hearing for the next morning. If no other evidence is presented that causes you to change your mind, the suspension stands.

Standard 6: *to understand, respond to, and influence the larger political, social, economic, legal, and cultural context*

1. A student tells his teacher that another student has a weapon in his backpack. He states that the student showed it to him during passing. The teacher informs the principal immediately about the allegation. What should the principal do?

A. Ask the student how he knows that the boy has a weapon in his backpack.

B. Have a security officer remove the student with the weapon from class and search his backpack; if no weapon is found, send him back to class.

C. Contact the police immediately.

D. Search his backpack; if no weapon is found, search his person and locker.

Answer: D

Explanation:
Allegations about weapons are very serious matters and should be dealt with immediately. The school has a legal right to search a student's locker and backpack. When there is sufficient reason to believe that a student has a weapon on his person, a physical search may take place. Call the police immediately if a weapon is found. Notify the Superintendent as well. Interview and make note of students who may have witnessed the incident or seen the weapon.

2. A newspaper reporter contacts the principal to discuss recent fights between students that have taken place in and around school grounds. The reporter wants to use a statement from the principal as part of an upcoming article about increased gang activity in schools. What should the principal do?

A. Inform the reporter that the school has begun programs to deal with gangs, character education, and anti-bullying.

B. The principal should decline the invitation to speak with the reporter, direct him to the Superintendent for a statement, and inform the Superintendent of the reporter's inquiry.

C. Invite the reporter to meet with the principal and his cabinet.

D. Refer the reporter to the local police for information.

Answer: B

Explanation:
The Superintendent is the person who should deal with the media when there is a controversial or potentially negative situation involving a school. Only discuss positive events directly with the media.

3. A parent informs the principal that she does not want her child exposed to instruction or textbooks that deal with the theory of evolution because it is not what the Bible teaches. Her child's class is learning about Darwin's Theory of Evolution this week. How does the principal handle this situation?

A. Have the student removed from the class when evolution is discussed.

B. Inform the parent that since the students are required to know this theory for the Regents exam that the child must stay in class.

C. Tell the parent that her child is not responsible for this work since it contradicts the Bible.

D. Notify the parent that it is her right to have her child removed from class during this lesson but she is responsible for this theory on tests.

Answer: D

Explanation:
Students are responsible for work that is part of the district's curriculum and the state's learning standards. A parent has the right to have a child removed during instruction that contradicts family religious beliefs. Notify the parent that the child will be removed but the youngster is responsible for the information taught when it is given on an exam.

4. A teacher who does not have a homeroom or first period class is late almost every day. When you, the newly appointed principal, confront her, she states that she has a childcare problem and has to drive her child to school every day. She cannot get to work at 7:30 A.M.; she arrives around 8:20 A.M. daily. How do you respond to this teacher?

A. Inform her that she has to be in work at 7:30 A.M. contractually and that she has to work out her childcare problem immediately.

B. Make sure that the teacher never has a homeroom or a first period class so that her childcare situation can be addressed.

C. Allow her to arrange with her colleagues to cover her class in case she is not going to be there in time for her first class.

D. Ask the Superintendent to transfer her to an elementary school that has a later starting time for teachers and students.

Answer: A

Explanation:
Teachers have a responsibility to arrive at work at or before the appointed time. The teacher's collective bargaining agreement states the number of hours and minutes worked and the district or school designates those hours. Principals should not make this accommodation for teachers who cannot get to work on time. If the principal did not give this teacher a homeroom and allowed on-going lateness, the administrator would not be treating all teachers in an equitable manner.

5. A teacher reports to the principal that a cleaner frequently smells as if he has alcohol on his breath. As principal, how would you proceed?

A. Ask the Head Custodian to investigate.

B. Send the cleaner home immediately.

C. Meet with the cleaner and the Head Custodian.

D. Make a determination if the cleaner is intoxicated.

Answer: D

Explanation:
Allegations must be investigated immediately. If the cleaner is determined to be intoxicated, send him home and notify the Superintendent. The Superintendent will decide how to proceed. If the cleaner has alcohol on his breath upon arrival at school and appears to be performing his duties in a normal manner, meet with him and tell him that he cannot have alcohol on his breath while working in a school.

6. For the past few weeks, students have been pulling the fire alarm as a joke. False alarms are occurring two to three times per day. Teachers are complaining that they are losing valuable instructional time each time they have to vacate the building. As principal, what is your course of action?

A. Remind the staff that the building must be vacated every time a fire alarm goes off.

B. Notify the staff to disregard the bells and continue their instruction because you will announce a real emergency or a fire drill.

C. Station teachers near every fire alarm box so that students cannot pull the handle and cause a false alarm.

D. Interview students to find out if they know who is pulling the alarm.

Answer: A

Explanation:
When a fire alarm sounds, the building must be evacuated. The only exception is when it is announced to disregard the alarm before it goes off due to testing or repair.

7. A father comes to the office and asks to speak with his son. Your secretary tells you, the principal, about the father's request but mentions that there is an order of protection barring the father from any school contact with his child. What do you tell this parent?

A. Arrange a supervised visit with the Guidance Counselor in attendance.

B. Call the mother and get her permission for the father to speak to his son.

C. Phone the district's lawyer for advice.

D. Inform the father that he cannot have any contact with his son in school.

Answer: D

Explanation:
An order of protection must be carried out to its fullest extent. A copy of the order should be on file at the school. If the court order prevents a parent from seeing a child, the parent must leave the building. If the parent refuses, contact the police immediately.

8. You receive a phone call from the principal of a school in another state asking for academic, behavioral, and special education records for a student who just left your school. He would like you to fax them to him as soon as possible. As a principal, how do you respond to this request?

A. Have your secretary fax them to him.

B. Send them to the school through the mail.

C. Ask the principal for a written request.

D. Send all but the special education records to the school.

Answer: C

Explanation:
A written request (faxed or sent through the mail) is necessary before a school can release records to another school outside the district. Special education records cannot be released without parental consent. Inform the other principal that he needs a parental release in order to send the special education records.

District-based Multiple Choice Questions

Standard 1: *to develop, articulate, implement, and steward a vision of learning*

1. The Superintendent and the Assistant Superintendent for Instruction jointly review the Regents data from the high school, in particular, its Regents Mathematics scores over the last three years. The scores showed a marked decline in student performance. The Superintendent concluded that mathematics instruction was not rigorous enough and ordered the high school principal to increase the number of mathematics instructional periods per week. What conclusion can you draw from this scenario?

A. Increasing the number of instructional periods will definitely improve mathematics performance.

B. The Superintendent and Assistant Superintendent should charge the principal with the responsibility of investigating and providing a plan of action about declining student performance.

C. The Superintendent should force the principal to resign.

D. The Assistant Superintendent should take charge of the mathematics program at the high school.

Answer: B

Explanation:
Improving instruction should begin at the school level and involve teachers and administrators jointly in investigating the issues and providing appropriate remedies to the problem. By imposing a solution, the shared ownership by the staff is greatly diminished, and opportunity for success is likewise reduced. A timeline would be appropriate.

2. Due to an increase in the number of altercations throughout the school district, the Assistant Superintendent for Instruction was charged with the responsibility of investigating character education programs for district adoption. After researching a variety of character education programs, what is the next step in this process?

A. Establish a district committee for character education including administrators, teachers, support staff, and parents.

B. Meet with principals to describe programs initially reviewed.

C. Meet with the Superintendent and have him mandate the desired program.

D. Send a memorandum to the guidance counselors to pick the best program from the list included in the memorandum.

Answer: A

Explanation:
To implement a character education program, a district-wide committee should be established including a variety of constituencies for input. Any program selected would then reflect the belief systems of the various groups within the school district and be more easily accepted for implementation.

3. At a recent meeting of district and school based administrators, the Superintendent announced that he was starting an initiative on strategic planning. The Superintendent explained that strategic planning involved long-range decision-making so that the district functioning could be envisioned in the future. The Superintendent handed out a document, which listed long-term goals for the school district over the next five years. The document explained the Superintendent's vision. The Superintendent asked for discussion of his goals and a vote of adoption. What's wrong?

A. The Superintendent laid out the future goals for the district as he saw them. It is his responsibility as district leader to do so.

B. Strategic planning should involve a variety of constituencies, which were never given the opportunity to help develop the district's future goals.

C. The administrators were never asked for their opinion about developing long-term goals.

D. All of the above

Answer: D

Explanation:
Strategic planning involves a number of constituencies over time in developing long-term goals. The Superintendent acting alone only provides one perspective for the district over time. By involving other constituencies, a more realistic and balanced look at the future would be attained. With multi-constituent consensus, change could then be institutionalized.

4. The Superintendent is an advocate for shared decision-making and established shared decision-making committees with lots of latitude for operation at each of the district's schools. One of the responsibilities the committees had was preparing schools' budgets. Thus, in turn, each committee presented its school's budget for the Superintendent's consideration. However, one elementary school decided that monies should be put aside for an assistant principal's salary line because the committee felt there were too many children for just the principal to handle. The Superintendent told the committee that in some cases like this, "the Superintendent makes the decision and shares it with the committee." What's wrong with this issue?

A. Nothing

B. The Superintendent expressed a desire to have a committee make school budgetary decisions and then vetoed its decision.

C. The Superintendent gave too much power to the committees.

D. The shared decision-making committee abused its power.

Answer: B

Explanation:
Shared decision-making is a commitment to having decisions that affect a school's functioning take place at a level that would most directly affect teaching and learning. A shared decision making committee includes a variety of constituencies within a school community including administrators, teachers, parents, students (in some cases), and support personnel. All of these people work for the betterment of their school. If the Superintendent did not give shared decision making committee parameters to deal with personnel issues, then the committee's actions are valid. If the committee gave due diligence to researching and justifying the need for an assistant principal's budget line, then the Superintendent who gave them their charge, without qualification, should give serious consideration to the committee's decision to the Board of Education.

5. A parent complains to the principal that technology is not well used in the building. In addition, the parent states that the equipment is outdated. The parent wants to know what the principal's plans are to obtain up-to-date equipment and get teachers to use it more with students. How should the principal proceed?

A. Survey your staff to find out how technology is being used in each of their classrooms.

B. Speak with the Director of Technology about upgrading computers.

C. Have each chairperson send the principal a description of how technology is being used in his or her department.

D. Suggest that the parent discuss the matter with the Director of Technology.

Answer: D

Explanation:
In most districts, building administrators do not make decisions about computer purchases. This falls under the jurisdiction of the district's Director of Technology or Assistant Superintendent for Instruction. The building administrator should acknowledge the parent's concern and suggest that computer purchases be discussed with the appropriate decision makers. Call the person at the district level that has this responsibility and let that person know to expect a call from this parent.

Standard 2: *to promote the success of all students, promote a positive school culture, provide an effective instructional program, apply best practice to student learning, and design comprehensive professional growth plans for staff*

1. The Superintendent's vision is to create small learning communities in each school focused on the area of children's literacy, something of great interest to the Superintendent. The Superintendent issues a memorandum to building principals to disseminate to the staff information about the creation of these learning communities around literacy. Without doubt, there is resistance. What is one reason that you might attribute to resistance?

A. The principals and teachers were not as interested in participating in learning communities.

B. The staff ignored it because the Superintendent ordered it.

C. The principals did not believe in change.

D. The Superintendent did not gather support for the change process by enlisting support of the principals and discussing learning communities with constituencies.

Answer: D

Explanation:
In order for change to take place, the Superintendent could consult and discuss proposed changes with a variety of constituencies in the district, including but not limited to administrators, teachers, parents, and Board of Education members.

2. The Assistant Superintendent for Curriculum and Instruction set up a meeting with the district's principals to review the professional development agenda for the upcoming school year. At the meeting, the Assistant Superintendent indicated that an extensive agenda for the use of professional development days has been planned already for the upcoming school year. How do you think the principals responded?

A. The principals indicated their delight with not having to participate in the planning and implementation of programming for staff development days.

B. The principals indicated their displeasure with the plan because their staffs were not involved in the planning and implementation of programming for staff development days.

C. The Assistant Superintendent indicated that he was following the district's professional development plan in establishing the current program.

D. None of the above

Answer: B

Explanation:
Professional development is most effective when a needs assessment is conducted to determine the needs and types of professional development teachers and other staff required to optimize instruction and meet the mission, vision, and goals of the district.

3. A culture exists within the school district in which teachers excessively take off days from work on Mondays and Fridays. The Superintendent issued a memorandum indicating that teachers taking off on Mondays and/or Fridays without a doctor's note would be docked two days pay. Of the choices provided below, which choice would not be an option to reduce or change teacher absence in the school district?

A. The Superintendent would require a teacher and the district union representative to meet with him regarding the teacher's absence to set an example.

B. The Superintendent issues a memorandum to principals holding them responsible for teacher absence.

C. The Superintendent would speak at each school's faculty meeting encouraging teacher attendance.

D. The Superintendent offers a monetary incentive to teachers for good attendance.

Answer: B

Explanation:
The Superintendent's actions in choices A, C, and D seem plausible. However, it does not resolve the problem by holding principals responsible for something out of their control.

Standard 3: *to ensure management of the organization, operations, and resources for a safe, efficient, and effective learning environment*

1. The Director of Special Education receives a phone call from an irate parent who states that her classified resource room child has not received resource room services for the past three days because her child's teacher is being used as a substitute for absent classroom teachers. The Director tells the parent she will look into the matter and get back to her. What should the Director do first?

A. Telephone the principal to ascertain if the resource room teacher is being used as a daily substitute.

B. Issue a memorandum to principals stating the law indicates that resource room teachers may not be used as daily substitute teachers.

C. Go over to the school to see if the resource room teacher is being used as a daily substitute teacher.

D. Telephone the resource room teacher at home to find out from her what is going on.

Answer: A

Explanation:
The Director of Special Education should follow the chain of command and contact the building principal immediately to get a reasonable explanation to the issue. Making a visit to the school and speaking with the resource room teachers might also take place during a thorough investigation, but the first step should be speaking with the principal.

2. The Superintendent meets with the Council of Parents on a monthly basis to discuss issues that are of importance to parents and to present plans and programs the Superintendent wishes to share with the parents. At one monthly meeting, the parents brought up the issue of developing a new policy for their children to legally possess cell phones and other electronic devices in school. How should the Superintendent react to the request of the parent group?

A. Tell the parents to mind their own business and stick to bake sales and fundraisers.

B. The superintendent should tell the parents that he would write a new policy immediately for their consideration.

C. Ignore the parents' request.

D. The Superintendent should tell the parents than he would share their concern with the Board of Education since their demand would require developing a new policy.

Answer: D

<u>**Explanation:**</u>
Any policy developed must be approved by the Board of Education at a regularly scheduled public meeting. Moreover, in developing such a policy, input should be obtained from administrators and teachers who would have to deal with implementing the policy, to evaluate its potential impact on the instructional program and discipline within the schools. Cell phones may compromise or otherwise interfere with student safety and security issues.

3. Due to a midyear reduction in state aid, the Assistant Superintendent for Business must reduce spending within the school district. The Assistant Superintendent has several ideas, which he shared with the Superintendent, who shared them with the Board of Education. Budget cuts were announced at the next Board of Education meeting. Who was not included in developing the budget reduction?

A. Teachers

B. District and school based administrators

C. Non-teaching support personnel

D. All of the above

Answer: D

Explanation:
In order to achieve a budget reduction that would appropriately reduce spending across the district, input should be sought from a variety of constituencies, including, but not limited to teachers, administrators, support personnel, and other groups that would be directly affected by reducing the budget. Additionally, the Assistant Superintendent would also want to meet with the leaders of the various collective bargaining units within the district before developing a final plan. Reductions should be based upon the district's core value system and what it deems untouchable vs. what is less valued. The core should be easily understood by reading the district's mission statement. That could only happen through such collaboration. Even if some of the input is not honored, all parties would have been given the courtesy of being heard.

4. An eight-year-old third grade youngster brought a loaded 25-caliber pistol to school in his backpack. He took the gun out of the backpack and placed it in his desk so that he could show his friends what he had. His classroom teacher overheard a conversation about the gun and subsequently removed the weapon from the youngster's desk. The weapon was handed over to the principal who immediately called the Superintendent. What is the first step the Superintendent should take after receiving the phone call?

A. Suspend the youngster for one year.

B. Call the youngster's parent.

C. Tell the principal to call the police.

D. Have the principal bring the weapon to the Superintendent's office to see if it was real.

Answer: C

Explanation:
As per Project SAVE, once informed that a youngster was in possession of a weapon on school grounds, the principal must notify the police immediately. The Superintendent was correct in telling the principal to call the police immediately and then the principal could consult with the Superintendent about disciplinary procedures. All students would have been removed from the room and relocated until the police removed the weapon from the desk. Neither the teacher nor the principal should touch the weapon under any circumstances.

5. The Director of Athletics wanted to develop an acceptable grade policy for student athletes. He thought that students must maintain at least a "C" average to participate in sports. How should he first proceed?

A. Send a memorandum to the principals implementing this policy.

B. Discuss the issue with the high school principals and come to an agreement as to an appropriate academic eligibility average.

C. Discuss the issue with the coaches.

D. Discuss the issue with student athletes to see if they could maintain a "C" average.

Answer: C

Explanation:
Before implementing a grade eligibility policy, the Athletic Director should first discuss the issue with his coaches to see the potential impact on sports programs. The next steps up the ladder would be discussions with the building principal, then the Assistant Superintendent for Instruction, and finally the Superintendent.

6. The Director of State and Federal Programs for a medium-sized urban school district disburses and monitors No Child Left Behind funding to qualified schools. One of the schools submits a request for the purchase of 30 I Pods with the justification that the I Pods would be used to help students study for their midterms and finals. What steps might you take?

A. Authorize the expenditure and monitor its effect.

B. Do not authorize the expenditure because you anticipate that the I Pods will be stolen.

C. Authorize the expenditure and suggest the purchase of additional I Pods in case of theft.

D. Do not authorize the expenditure because you know that students cannot concentrate on their studies while music is playing.

Answer: A

Explanation:
The school requested funding for a project that they felt was worthy of funding. If their application and justification was adequate, then the Director should monitor this expenditure and see if it affects student achievement.

7. The Athletic Director notifies you, the Superintendent, that he heard a rumor that some of the high school athletes are buying steroids at a local gym. What action do you take first?

A. Tell the Athletic Director that it is his responsibility to deal with this situation.

B. Notify the Superintendent about the alleged steroid use.

C. Inform the parents that their children are using steroids.

D. Contact the police.

Answer: D

Explanation:
The principal should contact the police and then notify the Superintendent about the alleged use of illegal substances at the local gym. The principal should cooperate with the police in their investigation.

Standard 4: *to collaborate with families and community members, to respond to diverse community interests and needs, and to mobilize community resources*

1.   A community based committee dealing with minority issues and concerns approached the Superintendent for a meeting about closing the minority achievement gap. What first step should the Superintendent make prior to the meeting?

A. Send a memorandum to the Board of Education dismissing the concerns of the committee as unfounded.

B. Set up a meeting with the Assistant Superintendent for Instruction and the Director of Evaluation to look at the achievement of minority students over the last three years.

C. Meet with the committee dismissing their concerns.

D. Send a memorandum to the Board of Education describing the minority achievement gap and what you intend to do about it.

Answer: B

Explanation:
The first step of many to deal with a community-based committee on minority achievement would be to establish the pertinent facts regarding minority achievement across the school district. The Superintendent should meet with the Assistant Superintendent and the Director of Evaluation to examine the achievement gap, if any, and determine where it exists among the district schools.

2. The school fields are available for use by members of the community on weekends. A sign is posted at each field with rules for appropriate use of the field, which includes use for athletic events and games, team sports, and individual sporting activities. The sign clearly indicates that no motorized vehicles are permitted in the field. A homeowner whose property is adjacent to the school's field takes his six-year-old son for a ride on his go-kart around the school field every weekend. School security reports that he refuses to leave saying, "I pay taxes and I can use the field on weekends. I'm not bothering anyone." You get the name and address of this community member. How do you proceed as Director of Buildings and Grounds?

A. Wait for the homeowner on the weekend and reprimand him while he is riding on the go-kart.

B. Suspend the homeowner's son.

C. Call the police and have him arrested for trespassing.

D. Explain to the homeowner that a sign is clearly posted prohibiting use of motorized vehicles in the field and failure to abide by the regulation will result in police involvement.

Answer: D

Explanation:
Explain to the homeowner that a sign is clearly posted prohibiting use of motorized vehicles in the field. Keeping positive community relations is an important function of a successful administrator. Suggest that this is a safety issue. In addition, many people use the field for a variety of activities and the use of a go-kart would endanger those people using the field.

3. Teachers have always attended evening and Saturday Parent Organization events. The teachers are now without a contract and refuse to attend these events. The Parent Organization comes to see you, the Superintendent, very upset and wants you to get the teachers to attend. What is your first step?

A. Tell the non-tenured teachers that they have to attend.

B. Meet with the union representative to ask for her cooperation.

C. Inform the teachers that their attendance at these events is a "past practice" and that you expect them to be present.

D. Explain to the Parent Organization president that the teachers attended these events voluntarily and cannot be forced to attend if they choose not to.

Answer: D

Explanation:
Although teachers attend many Parent Organization functions on their own time, they are not contractually bound to do so. Teachers (with a few exceptions) have the right to discontinue this practice at will. Explain to the Parent Organization president that there is a strong possibility that teachers will resume this practice after contract negotiations are resolved. Inform the Superintendent of what has transpired.

Standard 5: *to act with integrity, fairness, and in an ethical manner*

1. The Director of Personnel prepared a posting for a vacancy for an elementary school assistant principalship. The posting indicated that resumes were to be forwarded to the Director of Personnel. At the appropriate time, the Director reviewed the resumes for the following criteria: certification and experience, gender, age, and nationality. Which one of the criteria is appropriate to examine?

A. Certification and experience

B. Gender

C. Age

D. Nationality

Answer: A

Explanation:
It is discriminatory to classify applicants for a position by their age, gender, and race/nationality under the Equal Employment Opportunity Commission.

2. The Assistant Superintendent for Business regularly reviewed expenditures made by all district fiscal responsibility centers. One claim for reimbursement included travel expenses for a district employee attending an approved conference. The claim requested that the district reimburse the employee for dinner for $185. What should the Assistant Superintendent do?

A. Authorize the claim be paid since the employee's conference was approved by the Superintendent.

B. Deny the claim be paid since the employee spent more for dinner than legally allowed to reimburse.

C. Authorize the claim be paid after speaking with the Superintendent.

D. Deny the claim be paid because the employee did not complete the appropriate paperwork for a large reimbursement.

Answer: B

Explanation:
The State Education Department issues guidelines for reimbursement for expenditures while attending conferences, with a fixed rate for reimbursement for meals. These rates are confirmed annually and may be regionally weighted depending upon the location of the expense.

3. Just before the football season starts, a vacancy has arisen for an assistant football coaching position. The Director of Personnel wants to post the vacancy immediately but the Athletic Director indicates that he has someone to fill the vacancy. What is the next step?

A. The Director of Personnel should let the Athletic Director fill the vacancy.

B. The Director of Personnel should ignore the request of the Athletic Director and post the vacancy immediately.

C. The Athletic Director should ignore the Director of Personnel and fill the vacancy with his personal selection.

D. The Athletic Director should tell his candidate to apply immediately for the vacancy.

Answer: B

Explanation:
All vacancies for extra compensation positions must be posted immediately so that all potential applicants could have an opportunity to apply for that position. However, an approved substitute may be placed in the position and may apply for the vacancy.

Standard 6: *to understand, respond to, and influence the larger political, social, economic, legal, and cultural context*

1. A Superintendent was concerned about the students and teachers communicating with each other on social networks. The Superintendent contacted the district's lawyer for a legal opinion. Which response indicates the best possible action the Superintendent might take?

A. The Superintendent indicated that nothing could be done because it was not the district's responsibility.

B. The Superintendent posted an email to staff and students that inappropriate behavior would not be tolerated.

C. The Superintendent, in consultation with the district's lawyer, issued strict guidelines for use of social networks by teachers in communicating with children.

D. The Superintendent banned the use of social networks by blocking access to them on school computer systems.

Answer: C

Explanation:
According to school attorneys, the best way to prevent abuse of electronic media is to establish both student and employee codes of conduct, to promptly investigate cyber bullying and involve the authorities in all such investigations. Teachers that use a social network to communicate with students and then post something strikingly inappropriate could face disciplinary action, dismissal, and loss of license.

2. The Superintendent became fast friends with a Board of Education member over the first three years in office. One day the board member came to the Superintendent and asked for a favor. The district posted a vacancy for a Director of Community Relations. The board member requested that the Superintendent interview his daughter for the position. What does the Superintendent do next?

A. Tell the Board of Education member that it is unethical to interview a relative of any board member for a district position.

B. Tell the board president that he would interview the candidate only if the board member resigned since that would pose no conflict of interest.

C. Have the district's lawyer advise the whole Board of Education about the rules and regulations pertaining to hiring relatives of Board of Education members.

D. Withdraw the vacancy for the Director of Community Relations.

Answer: C

Explanation:
Although it might be unethical to hire the daughter of a Board of Education member within the school district in which the board member serves, it is not illegal. The attorney for the district should advise that if the individual got through the screening process with no influence from the Board of Education or Superintendent, that particular Board of Education member would have to abstain from voting.

3. After an affluent school district passed its budget, the Superintendent gave the Director of Technology a large allocation of funds to upgrade the district's telephone system. The Board of Education required the Director to report to the board the status of the telephone upgrade plan. At that meeting, a board member asked the Director what phone system he intended to purchase; the board member indicated that he knew someone in the telephonic business that could get a system installed cheaply. What is the best response to the board member?

A. The Director should tell the board member that his friend could NOT submit a bid because he is a friend of a board member.

B. The Director would be sending out a request for bids and the board member's friend could submit a bid along with other companies.

C. The Director should request a private meeting with the board member to see how cheaply his friend could install the system.

D. The Director should ask the Assistant Superintendent for Business who his favorite phone company is, and then contact them for phone system installation.

Answer: B

Explanation:
There are strict purchasing guidelines established by the State Education Department and the Office of General Services for the large scale purchasing by school districts statewide. The Director of Technology must prepare a RFB, Request for Bid, outlining the scope and breadth of the require work district-wide and the types of equipment to be purchased. Bids must be publicly posted for prospective bidders and opened in public to avoid any possibility of impropriety.

4. The district Director of Personnel has prepared a file for the Superintendent of all teachers coming up for tenure during the current school year, including their observations, attendance and positive recommendations from their building principals. The Superintendent reviewed the file and recommended that one teacher on the list will be denied tenure.

A. The Superintendent can recommend the termination of untenured teachers anytime before their tenure date with appropriate notice of termination and due process.

B. The Superintendent does not have to consult with the union leadership about recommending the termination of an untenured teacher.

C. The Superintendent can recommend the termination of an untenured teacher without the support of the building principal.

D. All of the above

Answer: D

Explanation:
An untenured teacher can be dismissed without cause during the three-year probationary period, as long as the reason for dismissal does not violate the civil rights of the employee, i.e. termination is not based on religion, race, age discrimination, gender, etc.

5. The Director of Personnel posted a vacancy for the civil service position of groundskeeper. Letters of application were received from applicants in a timely basis. One day after the deadline for letters of application, a Board of Education member personally brings a letter of application to your office for this vacancy and tells you that this is his cousin. The Superintendent requests that you forward the applications to his office after your initial review of qualifications. What do you do?

A. Send all letters of application to the Superintendent.

B. Send all letters of application except the Board of Education member's cousin.

C. Meet with the Superintendent, describing the circumstance involving the board member, and hand the Superintendent that person's letter of application.

D. Call the Superintendent, apprise him of the board member's request and ask for direction with regard to this candidate's application.

Answer: D

Explanation:
It is the responsibility of the Director of Personnel to point out this issue to the Superintendent and let him give you next steps. Most school districts have policies about employing relatives of Board of Education members. In making the Superintendent aware of this situation, the Director has met his ethical obligation.

6. A parent wrote a letter to the Assistant Superintendent for Business requesting that her children receive free lunch because she lost her job as a real estate agent for premier homes in the community and was forced to take a job as a real estate agent at a lower paying agency.

A. Send her a letter indicating that she is not eligible because she is still working.

B. Send her a letter indicating that her request is approved.

C. Send her a free and reduced lunch application along with eligibility guidelines for free and reduced lunch.

D. Forward her request to the county Department of Social Services.

Answer: C

Explanation:
Under the law, every parent is eligible to apply for free and reduced lunch program. Successful applicants must meet federal guidelines for income eligibility for free and/or reduced lunch.

Preparing for Educational Leadership

7. The president of the Parent Organization writes a letter to the Superintendent indicating that their council took a vote that the district could save money by terminating the school bus program at the elementary level. She said that the parents would gladly drop off and pick up their children from elementary school daily. How should the Superintendent respond to the letter?

A. Send a reply that in order to change the district's busing policy, the Superintendent would have to place an item on the Board of Education's monthly agenda for action.

B. Send a reply that in order to change the district's busing policy, the Superintendent would have to request an item be placed on that ballot to be voted by the community as part of the annual budget vote.

C. Send a reply that in order to change the district's busing policy, the Superintendent would have to consult with the principal's of the elementary schools.

D. Ignore the letter completely.

Answer: B

Explanation:
In order to change any busing policy, a public vote is required.

142

8. The Superintendent was informed that a parent chaperone on an overnight trip was having a liaison with one of the female teacher chaperones on the trip. They were seen drinking in the hotel bar and leaving the hotel together. Another teacher told her building principal upon return from the trip that this took place. The building principal immediately called the Superintendent. What should be done about the employee and parent?

A. Tell the teacher that her conduct is inexcusable.

B. Have the teacher put the parent on the phone and advise him that he has to stop seeing the teacher.

C. Give the teacher a copy of the rules of conduct for professionals and require her to resign.

D. Conduct an investigation, get witness statements and refer the matter to the district's legal counsel for action against the teacher employee.

Answer: D

Explanation:
A teacher who violates a district code of conduct must be accountable for her actions and due process must be provided. Remember the phrase: "you are innocent until proven guilty." It is incumbent upon the Superintendent to meet with the teacher along with her union representative to ascertain if this incident took place. Likewise, the Superintendent must obtain statements from other adults on the trip to corroborate the allegation. Legal action could be taken if corroborated by witness statements if the teacher violated the "moral turpitude" clause in the district's code of conduct.

9. You have been informed that one of the students in the district lost a parent due to infectious meningitis. The parent group wants the child barred from school because the youngster may be a health threat to others. As Superintendent, what is your next action?

A. Assign the student to home instruction while you are gathering information about the disease.

B. Discuss the matter with the Board of Education before deciding what to do with the student.

C. Request medical clearance before allowing the child to attend school.

D. Let the school nurse decide whether the student can return to school.

Answer: C

Explanation:
Medical clearance is needed from the child's physician to permit the child to attend school because of exposure to a contagious disease. It is a good idea to have the district nurse or attending physician prepare information about meningitis and disseminate it to all parents to alleviate any concerns about their children's exposure to the disease.

Chapter 8

Work Products

Chapter 8

School-based Work Product

Fairview Middle School

One day in July, the Fairview Board of Education, upon recommendation of the Superintendent, appointed a new principal to Fairview Middle School, Ms. Madelyn Torres. Ms. Torres was told that her administrative team consisted of the three assistant principals, a full-time dean of students, and herself. Fairview is an urban middle school with a student population of 1000 students. When the school opened some 70 years ago, its student population was predominantly white. Today the population has changed, with the student population 100% Hispanic. Fairview's attendance area includes some of the highest crime rates in the city. As a result, middle class families who were previously connected to the school have moved out of the community. The current median income for a family of four now living in this community is below the poverty level.

Fairview Middle School experiences issues with discipline, attendance, and achievement. As a result, the Superintendent, with support from the Board of Education, directed the new principal to restructure Fairview into smaller, more manageable mini-schools. He ordered Mrs. Torres to implement the mini-schools model as quickly as possible and bring the school under control, eliminate negative press, improve school climate, and change the culture of chaos into three small learning communities. The Superintendent believes that there will be a marked improvement in the overall school climate as well as student achievement when this change takes place.

Parents, students, and community members feel that the school is unsafe due to the large enrollment and the previous administration's policy of not equitably implementing the discipline policy. Moreover, students are at-risk and not succeeding academically. The school has a poor attendance rate. The bottom line is Fairview's climate is toxic. The climate has deteriorated to the point where teachers lock themselves in their classrooms and rarely connect with students and colleagues. Parents believe that their children are not connected to the school. Teachers feel isolated.

Ms. Torres believes that the Fairview community has potential. There is a pool of talented youngsters and many dedicated, competent teachers who have just given up because of frustration. Ms. Torres has been given autonomy to be as creative as she likes, but the bottom line is to restore order and create a climate in which teachers can teach and students can learn.

Preparing for Educational Leadership

Document #1: School Fact Sheet

Fairview Middle School

- There are 1000 students attending Fairview Middle School, and approximately 90% of the students receive free or reduced lunch.

- The school is a large building sitting on one square city block.

- The school has a veteran teaching staff with an average length of service of over 15 years; the student teacher ratio is 25:1 while the student administrator ratio is 200:1.

- A great many of the students are classified (over 20%) special education, with special education the largest department in the school with 25 teachers.

- There are large numbers of students who are English language learners. (23%)

- Over 20% of the students are academically at-risk; the average daily attendance rate is below 75%

- There are no after school activities and clubs-most have been eliminated because of security issues.

- There are a high number of pupil suspensions, 395 last year, with 41 Superintendent suspensions. (Suspension Rate 30%)

State Assessment Results

	Level 4	Level 3	Level 2	Level 1
ELA				
Year 1	2%	10%	74%	14%
Year 2	3%	9%	73%	15%
Year 3	3%	12%	71%	14%
Mathematics				
Year 1	2%	9%	74%	15%
Year 2	2%	11%	71%	16%
Year 3	3%	12%	72%	13%

Level 4: Advanced, Level 3: Proficient, Level 2: Making Some Progress, Level 1: Making Little or No Progress

Document #2: Principal's Letter to the Faculty

Dear Colleagues:

The Superintendent, with the support of the Board of Education, has mandated that we restructure our Fairview Middle School into small, nurturing learning communities (mini-schools) by the start of the following school year.

The concept of mini-schools was developed in an urban school system like ours about 30 years ago as school districts struggled to deal with large dysfunctional schools having unhealthy climates and a high number of academically and socially at-risk youngsters with less than proficient test scores. Mini-schools recognize that small schools provide a nurturing environment, are safe and caring, and instructionally challenging. In a mini-school, a team of teachers work with a group of students in core academic subjects and those related to the mini-school's theme. Classroom instruction is dynamic and includes career exploration, community service, and professional mentoring. There are many themes for mini-schools. Some of the more successful themes are centered on transportation, medicine, business, entertainment, law and law enforcement, graphic design, and leadership.

Typically, a mini-school may include 100–400 students. Block scheduling is usually employed to provide flexibility with implementing an integrated curricula. Mini-schools have succeeded in increasing student achievement and attendance rates by:

- Students are immersed in learning that is focused around a set of core values.
- Staff members are nurturing and remain with the students for the duration of their school experience.
- Businesses, colleges, and community organizations are involved in mini-school environments.

I understand that this impending reorganization will increase your anxiety. Therefore, I would like to meet with you this Thursday, at 3:15 p.m. in the school auditorium. At that time, you can learn more about this initiative. While the session is not mandatory, it would be helpful for everyone to attend.

Very truly yours,

Madelyn Torres
Principal, Fairview Middle School

Document 3: Principal's Memo to the Superintendent

To: Superintendent of Schools

From: Ms. Torres, Principal, Fairview Middle School

Date: September 15

Re: Restructuring Fairview Middle School

This memo is to update you about my vision for the mini-schools model that we will implement next school year. In consultation with faculty, we have developed objectives for mini-schools:

- To create schools within a school environment that nurture academic and social emotional development of middle school youngsters.
- To provide a cadre of teachers who remain with their students throughout their school experience.
- To immerse students in an integrated thematic instructional program that enhances their self-esteem.
- To provide youngsters with college, community, and/or corporate mentors.
- To provide mini-schools with financial and technical resources from the business community.

We have determined that mini-schools depend on a group of teachers to teach core subjects that integrates each school's thematic focus within its curriculum. We recognize that extensive professional development will be needed and I have discussed with staff that teachers will work collegially through coordinated planning times provided in the new schedule to launch their mini-school. Additionally, we are counting on consultants from universities to work with teachers on developing each mini-school's theme. We understand that mini-schools do not generally require the assignment of extra teachers, but an additional staff member may be required to serve as each school's curriculum and community liaison coordinator.

I am excited, as the new principal of Fairview Middle School, to work with my staff and our school community on ideas that I hope will affect generations yet to come.

Preparing for Educational Leadership

Directions: The three documents provided relate to the situation described. Read all documents and the school's description carefully and respond to each of the following questions:

Questions:

1. Give one strength of Fairview Middle School. What evidence would you use to support this determination? What strategy might you use to enhance this strength?

2. List two weaknesses of Fairview Middle School. What evidence would you use to support this determination?

3. Explain why knowing this information might be helpful for school improvement.

4. What should Ms. Torres consider in preparing a short-term plan of action that would ensure the successful implementation of the mini-schools model?

5. How should the principal improve the school's climate to restructure the school?

6. Whom should the principal enlist in responding to these issues?

7. The principal has been given a mandate to bring order and structure to the operation of the school and transform the school's culture from one of chaos to one of improved learning. Describe specific strategies and give specific benchmarks that you would point to in this undertaking.

Responses:

1. Give one strength of Fairview Middle School. What evidence would you use to support this determination? What strategy might you use to enhance upon this strength?

Fairview does have some strengths:

- Senior staff of dedicated teachers
  Document #1: Fact Sheet indicates that average length of service for teachers is 15 years. Senior staff brings to the table a variety of strengths. Their expertise in subject areas and their dedication to student learning are invaluable assets.

- Recognition that students' learning is important for students to be successful
  The school's description and Document #1 provide evidence that there are a small number of students for which learning is important. This cadre of students would serve as a starting

153

point for establishing mini-schools. Perhaps a survey of students and their parents would help clarify what mini-schools the community desired and how the schools might look after restructuring.

- The physical plant is large and can accommodate a number of mini-schools
  Document #1: The Fact Sheet indicates that the school is a large building, on a footprint of one square city block. Buildings of this size can easily be converted into mini-schools.

2. List two weaknesses of Fairview Middle School. What evidence would you use to support this determination?

Fairview has weaknesses, some of which include:

- Low attendance rate
  A low attendance rate is confirmed in Document #1, which indicates that the attendance rate is only 75%.

- Disciplinary issues
  Disciplinary issues are confirmed in Document #1, which indicates a high level of violence exists in Fairview. There were 395 principal's suspensions and 41 Superintendent's suspensions last year. Moreover, all after school activities are banned. Additionally, the School Description includes a statement that teachers lock themselves into their classrooms and are frustrated with the school's climate. The description also includes a statement that the school evidences a climate of chaos, which correlates with disciplinary issues.

- Low academic achievement
  Low academic achievement is evident by examining Document #1 which indicates that significantly low numbers of students are making progress at Advanced or Proficient levels of achievement on State assessments in English language arts and mathematics over a three-year period.

3. Explain why knowing this information might be helpful for school improvement.

Fairview Middle School is dysfunctional; it displays all the factors that call for change. It is a school that is in desperate need of restructuring. The school has a toxic climate, one in which both teachers and students cannot function; teaching and learning is an insurmountable task. Its inhabitants have to be concerned with daily safety. These factors along with the potential displayed by a number of students, makes school improvement an imperative. As stated in the principal's memorandum to her staff, mini-schools provide a nurturing environment and are safe, caring, and instructionally challenging. Teams of teachers work with small groups of students over time in core subjects. Instruction is supplemented with related experiences. These factors can counter the culture of dysfunction and produce small functional learning environments.

4. What should Ms. Torres consider in preparing a short-term plan of action that would ensure the successful implementation of the mini-schools model?

In order to ensure success in implementing the mini-schools model, Ms. Torres should consider engaging a number of constituencies in the planning process.

Staff
- Support teachers so they can become creative problem solvers and assist classroom teachers to utilize their skills in developing the mini-school themes.

- Engage the whole staff in the reform process and stand in support of teachers.

- Create effective classroom observation processes, surveys, etc. to collect evidence of teacher strengths and areas of need, and use this data to make informed decisions about future teaching assignments in mini-schools and necessary professional development initiatives.

- Involve the entire school faculty in school planning to identify interim benchmarks as well as long-term goals needed and monitor their implementation.

Parents
- Establish a culture with a vision that includes participation by parents.

- Understand the concerns of parents through on-going communication, surveys, etc.

- Involve key parents in the design and implementation of the change process.

- Create a culture in the school that respects parents, welcomes them into the school, is sensitive to their diverse backgrounds, and encourages their on-going involvement.

- Create on-going communication between school and the parents that promotes two-way conversations (direct, print, telephone, electronic).

Local Business and Community Based Agencies:
- Facilitate participation in the planning and implementation by representatives of community based agencies, businesses, and universities.

- Create a communication process that will allow on-going dialogue between school and business leaders.

Media
- Establish positive relationships with the newspapers, local television, and radio stations by providing them with information about school accomplishments.

- Share with the media, with the approval of the Superintendent, information about the mini-schools model and how it would benefit students and community.

Students
- Build positive relationships with students to facilitate improved student achievement.

- Be fair and equitable with regard to student disciplinary procedures to facilitate a positive learning environment.

- Involve students in developing strategies for managing student behavior.

5. How should the principal improve the school's climate to restruc the school?

The principal should develop a more effective organization by improving the school's climate by first changing the skills, attitudes, and behaviors of the constituencies in the organization.

- Establish collaborative teams that work on changing behaviors and attitudes of staff and students.

- Encourage an atmosphere of trust.

- Share information that is in the best interest of the students.

- Make the school a comfortable place in which to work and learn for students and staff.

- Empower staff to become successful.

- Demonstrate skill in building and mending relationships by making people feel comfortable.

- Develop a set of firm, professional beliefs in collaboration with staff.

- Develop a strong sense of academic rigor.

- Communicate this vision to all stakeholders.

- Encourage risk taking, value ethical practices, and recognize others for their efforts while at the same time acknowledging mistakes along the way.

6. Whom should the principal enlist in responding to these issues?

The principal should enlist the following constituents in responding to these issues:

- Staff (both instructional and support)

- Parent community

- Business and community based agencies

- Media

- Students

7. The principal has been given a mandate to bring order and structure to the operation of the school and transform the school's culture from one of chaos to one of improved learning. Describe specific strategies and give specific benchmarks that you would point to in this undertaking.

The principal should implement a variety of strategies to bring order and organization to effectively transform the school:

- Communicate effectively with school and constituencies.

- Deal effectively and equitably with staff, parents and community-based agencies.

- Seek community support.

- Understand that it is imperative to communicate the school's mission and goals and the steps needed to reach them.

- Establish clear lines of communication regarding goals, performance, expectations, and feedback.

- Create a culture that fosters and maintains positive staff morale by perceiving the needs, concerns, and problems.

- Develop diplomacy in connecting adults and students from diverse backgrounds.

- Make decisions that based upon making logical and ethical conclusions, which are fair and equitable to all.

- Provide opportunities for the community to become active participants in school events, programs and organizations.

District-based Work Product

The Flanders School District

Overview

The Superintendent of the Flanders School District has the responsibility to align the district's budget with needs and taxpayer demands. The goal of this alignment is to assure that expenditures come under control in an ever-increasing demand for scarce resources. At a public meeting of the Board of Education in January, the Board president directed the Superintendent to come up with a plan to reduce the expense side of the budget by $1 million. The Superintendent discussed his dilemma with the Assistant Superintendent for Business. Together they came to the same conclusion: it was necessary to close one of the district's elementary schools to present a cost saving of that size to the Board of Education.

The Flanders School District is a suburban K–12 district with approximately 3000 students, educated in five elementary schools, two middle schools, and one high school. The Flanders School District is very progressive in terms of educational philosophy and offers a variety of courses and programs for its students.

The Assistant Superintendent for Business prepared an elementary school capacity chart in order to study the size and capacity of the district's elementary schools. In addition, the Assistant Superintendent prepared a cost analysis detailing the savings for closing one of the five elementary schools.

Chart #1: Size and Capacity of Elementary Schools

School	# Students	Capacity	% Utilization
1	310	420	74
2	280	340	82
3	400	510	78
4	330	410	80
5	200	300	67
Total	1520	1980	77

Chart #2: Potential Cost Savings

Operations:	$280,000
Staffing:	$720,000
Supplies and Materials:	$100,000
Total:	$1,100,000

Chart #3: School Population by Ethnicity

School	Pop.	%White	%Black	%Hispanic	%Asian	%.Ind.
1	310	43	25	27	5	0
2	280	39	31	29	1	0
3	400	51	19	21	9	0
4	330	29	29	32	9	1
5	200	32	29	28	11	0
Total	1520	39	27	27	7	0

Chart #4: Academic Performance of District Elementary Schools

English Language Arts, 2009

School	Pop.	%Level 4	%Level 3	%Level	%Level 1
1	310	16	57	20	7
2	280	19	43	29	9
3	400	23	64	12	1
4	330	18	65	17	0
5	200	20	57	19	4
Total	1520	19	58	19	4

Mathematics, 2009

School	Pop.	%Level 4	%Level 3	%Level 2	%Level 1
1	310	11	63	24	2
2	280	9	61	27	3
3	400	21	59	19	1
4	330	26	58	16	0
5	200	18	61	19	2
Total	1520	17	60	21	2

Document #1: Superintendent's Memorandum

Flanders School District
Memorandum

To: President, Board of Education, Flanders School District
From: Superintendent, Flanders School District
Date: February 15
Re: Closing of Elementary School

I am writing you to inform you of the potential cost savings versus detrimental effects of closing an elementary school. There are many factors to consider in closing a school, including condition of buildings, location of the school to be closed, safety for children going to and coming from schools, ethnicity of student population after consolidation, as well as the academic performance of all elementary school children.

In Chart #1 I have provided you with the elementary school populations and percent utilization so that you can judge for yourself the potential impact of closing one school on the utilization of the rest of the buildings.

In Chart #2 I have provided you with the potential cost savings of closing any elementary school. Cost savings are divided into operations, staffing, and supplies and materials. Operations include utility, heating, water, and maintenance costs. Staffing include principal, secretaries, guidance, custodial cleaners, head custodian, and teaching force reductions. Supplies and Materials include purchases necessary to run a school.

In Chart #3 I have provided you with the ethnic breakdown of each elementary school so that you understand that closing a building will affect the ethnic make-up of the remaining elementary schools.

In Chart #4 I have provided you with the academic performance of all district elementary schools. Be aware that by closing a building there is a potential negative impact on academic performance as you put more children in the other buildings.
I am available to discuss in detail the impact of closing an elementary school within the Flanders School District. I suggest that you study the

facts enclosed and that we meet in closed-door session in two weeks to discuss this issue.

Preparing for Educational Leadership

Document #2: Parents Council Letter Voicing Opposition to Closing an Elementary School

President, Board of Education
Flanders School District

March 1

Dear Mr. Board President:

On behalf of the parents of the Flanders School District, I am writing you to express our concerns about closing an elementary school. We have a variety of concerns that closing an elementary school will diminish our outstanding elementary level instructional program and squeeze our children to the other schools leaving them overcrowded. We believe that implementing this budget realignment will produce significant implications within an already demanding instructional program.

The Flanders School District has a long history of academic and social emotional success, in meeting the needs of every child. We moved into the Flanders School District because of the individualized attention provided our children in every school. Additionally, we cherish our children's experiences in the fine arts, music, physical education, drama, and other enrichment programs. It is our position, that this budget re-alignment will harm rather than benefit the academic performance and growth of our students.

We are requesting that the Board of Education consider other cost savings instead of closing an elementary school. We suggest looking at freezing expenditures over time as a viable alternative to closing a building. We stand ready to discuss this most pressing issue.

Sincerely,

President, Parents Council
The Flanders School District

Document #3: Letter from Flanders Teachers' Association

President, Board of Education
Superintendent
Flanders School District

March 15

Dear Mr. President:

We are officially writing to make our concerns known about the potential closing of an elementary school in our district. We believe that closing any elementary school would diminish the quality education offered to the children throughout the elementary schools. Invariably closing a school would increase the populations of the remaining schools, increase class size, and decrease the personalization and individualization that Flanders School District is known for.

We are aware that the budget building process for the next school year is not yet finished. In view of the pending budget re-alignment, we believe that closing a school would drastically change teaching demands on the district's teaching staff, and ultimately affect children's learning.

We would like to go on record opposing the closing of any district elementary school. We are available to meet with both of you at a mutually convenient time to establish a dialogue for developing budget alternatives to closing a school. Perhaps by lowering the administrator ratio, the district could achieve the same results.

Sincerely,

President
Flanders Teachers' Association

Document #4: Board of Education Minutes, April Public Meeting

Parents of the Flanders School District spoke out last night at a public meeting voicing their concerns about the closing a district elementary school and the potential of reduction of instructional services in the remaining elementary schools as a result of implementing the budget re-alignment.

Parents said the district's Superintendent informed them at a recent presentation that "it would be necessary to reduce supplementary services in order to provide time for mandated state requirements." Parents indicated that they fought hard to get these special enrichment programs for their children. They indicated that this is a step backwards. They were disappointed and angry.

The Board of Education president responded that the Board is caught in a no-win situation. The Board must be sure that the budget is aligned with taxpayer demands yet provide students with a world-class education so that they can perform well on the state assessments. The Board promised the parents that they would continue to address this issue.

Questions

Directions: *You are the Superintendent of Flanders School District. You have presented the Board of Education with four documents and charts related to the situation described. Read all documents and charts carefully and respond to each of the following questions:*

1. Describe how you would address the Board of Education's directive.
2. How would you involve the various constituencies in the district in the process?
3. What factors should you take into consideration in making a final recommendation to the Board of Education to close a building?

Response:

1. Describe how you would address the Board of Education's directive.

As Superintendent, I would take the following steps to comply with the directive of the Board of Education:

- Arrange for a meeting with the Board of Education to go over details of budget re-alignment.

- Share with the Board of Education specific issues related to closing a school, including condition of all elementary buildings, location of the school to be closed with regard to traffic flow, safety for children going to and coming from schools, e.g. street crossings, ethnicity of student population after consolidation, academic performance of all elementary school children.

- Provide the Board of Education with a detailed plan along with cost savings for closing an elementary school as well as other possible budget reduction scenarios, should they decide not to close a school.

- Share with the Board the latest data from educational research about the effect of closing a school on the climate of the district and educational performance of the children.

2. How would you involve the various constituencies in the district in the process?

The specific individuals/groups that would have responsibility in the implementation of the plan:

- The teachers will need to adjust their instruction in order to meet re-organized schools. They might have their teaching assignments changed and for some of them, will need to undergo staff development to learn new instructional methods of delivery.

- The building administrators will need to provide support to teachers as they move into their new teaching assignments. Administrators will have to modify building cultures because of the additional students and staff. Likewise, administrators will have to hand hold parents so that they can adjust to the school in which their child is educated.

- The Board of Education will need to support the school closing by providing additional funding that may be necessary for professional development and additional resources to accommodate the changes in the other elementary schools.

- The parents will need to adjust to the change in their child's assigned school so that they support their youngsters through a period of uncertainty.

- The students will be placed in new classrooms with students they are not familiar. They will exhibit higher levels of anxiety and stress, which need to be dealt with as part of the consolidation effort.

3. What factors should you take into consideration in making a final recommendation to the Board of Education to close a building?

As Superintendent, I would consider the following factors before making a final recommendation to the Board of Education regarding closing an elementary school:

- Ethnic breakdown of the elementary schools after consolidation

- Academic needs of students in all schools, including the provision of remedial services, special education services and services to English language learners.

- Staffing patterns of the elementary schools as a result of the consolidation effort.

- All safety concerns are addressed prior to consolidation.

- Transportation issues to and from school are addressed.